Bethany Rose's poem 'Pink' aired  over five million views, and h BBC1 had just under one millior poet and illustrator who writes to mental health, through to longing out performances across the world, with shows at The Poetry Cafe in Covent Garden, the Phoenix Club in the West-End, Le Chat Noir in Paris, and many more. Beth has done commissions for ITV, Amnesty International, The Courtauld Institute of Art and TEDx. Beth was also chosen to be one of Nationwide's 'Voice of the People', with her poem being aired on prime-time television for ITV.

NEON

Bethany Rose

Burning Eye

BurningEyeBooks
Never Knowingly
Mainstream

Supported using public funding by
ARTS COUNCIL
ENGLAND

LOTTERY FUNDED

This edition published by Burning Eye Books 2020

www.burningeye.co.uk

@burningeyebooks

Burning Eye Books
15 West Hill, Portishead, BS20 6LG

ISBN 978-1-911570-97-4

NEON

A.J -

Yours always -

Beth x x x

*For my magical and fabulous family, my
clever and kind therapist Caroline Midgley,
and of course, Cc: my home, my neon.*

CONTENTS

NITROGEN: a teenage poem

There was a blue door where we had our first kiss, but I forgot the key. We sat outside on the steps; my legs, skinny and adolescent, wrapped around your hips and spine. You tasted like Ribena and smoke. We let ourselves into a friend's house down the road, and we lay on a dirty mattress and you kissed my hips and made my skin burn and my heart implode. We had a year of tangles and landscapes, a year of horizons and bleached-out skies, of limes in our beers and pastel sunrises; legs dangling out from the top floor windowsill, whilst making our bare feet brush out the shapes of words that we did not yet know on each other's legs.

I couldn't afford shaving foam, so my legs always had razor rash – little cherry constellations climbing up my legs. You used to play join the dots on them with your fingers – like when you search for shapes in clouds, only this time the pictures came alive on my flesh. I miss being young – and when I say young, I mean acting in a way that can only happen when you don't know what grief tastes like yet; and even though sometimes your kisses were bitter, I didn't know the consequences that dancing with darkness could bring. Not then, as then was all about firsts: first kiss, first fire, first swallowing a solar system – and I guess you could say I was a late developer because even though I had done all those things before, I only really had ever felt them when I was with you. And today you got married, and I'm not a girl any more – and I thought it would feel different, but really, I'd give a lot for one more day to watch that sunrise from the angle that only came from loving you.

You were the girl that I once shared a packet of crisps with under a railway bridge whilst drinking whisky and talking about the ways in which we were going to be brave once we were grown up. You weren't right for me, but back then time was my lover – and you were my witness – and for that you will always make up part of my insides, and so I carry you around like nitrogen in my blood.

You were never the one, but you were part of me when I was larger than life, the moon in the sky, the absolute capital letter – and I should know better than to say this, but you – you were the beginning.

You were my beginning.

GEODE: AN INJURY POEM

I walked the balance beam every week until the week that I didn't
legs greeting the gym floor in an incident
my graze gasping in geode
crystals glittering and trapped in my body's code deep within
my knees like amethysts caught under my soft milk skin

I left PE early that day
with dark green paper towels soaked into the sting
pressed to the reminder of falling into myself
rather than outside something
the water droplets in a race down my legs
transparent like PVA glitter glue
running down like rivulets and landing
in the pooled lagoons of my buckled shoes

I close my eyes and imagine the moment just before I hit the floor
there is only now the time after the pain
and the time before
my skin's full stop after what went on outside
the classroom door and I pour
and I pull at the gravel caught in the crystals
and feel the pain bloom and shout
I open my lips and a whole hemisphere tumbles out
and tears get caught in the very changing room cubicles of me
there's bubble gum stuck under my cuticles
with fingerprints trapped forever in sour raspberry

I am a crystalline and sun-singed little thing
who hates wearing tights and hated singing
the alphabet (so I never got a gold star on the wall)
but I wasn't afraid of failing at all
I was more worried that my life was a continuation of a past life
like I was doing overtime in the hieroglyph of an afterlife
that I was just an Egyptian mummy
but thawed out and defrosted with my bandages ungluing
made to carry on to repent
for something I didn't even remember doing

I used to watch pencil shavings curl shyly into commas
in their sharpener ledges
clinging on to strips of pigment along their edges and under
I inhaled because when you're younger
everything smells like sugar and crayons side-by-side
sleeping softly in slumber
dolly mixtures and party rings balanced next to plastic tumblers

and I'm counting Greek before I play hide and seek
in alpha beta gamma delta
longing between my legs as I make static
on the silver of the helter-skelter
with my life filled with netball seasons and PE kit
and rainbow chalk and racket rust
the inside tomb of pencil cases filled with all that stationery dust
I wanted to hide away in their soft felt cradle
soft and mummified and do the zip up tight
and hold the erasers to say sorry for the fact
they never got to rub out what was right
what a responsibility
to get rid of every single mistake
sometimes I wonder
if we could gather all the erasers in the world
what stories all our wrongdoings could make

the next day I lined up for my tetanus injection
which I mixed up with Tetris
I thought they were going to put
the coloured bricks inside a syringe
to make me feel more like a rainbow
less like a shadow
less like a girl who was bullied
who once found a wasp at tennis in her apple Tango
I fainted clean on the floor and woke to a teacher
holding me tight like a hymn
underneath the climbing wall on the jungle gym
opia is a word that describes when someone looks at you

with tenderness and intensity in equal measure
and when I woke in her arms
that's the first time in my life
I felt less like cardboard and more like treasure
cherished and vulnerable all at the same time
like they could coexist
so I painted her a thank-you note
in primary pyramid lines with a kiss
and dreamed of her taking me in classes of just me
and I would be her little sequin and her gleam of a child prodigy
but the problem with dreams is that they leave you with no proof
and so you don't have much evidence
suddenly I understood what it was like to have an interior world
richer than your exterior reality
and what it was like to bridge that fence
suddenly I understood
why learning about longitude and latitude
was important in geography
because it meant I could finally map the place
where I felt like I was right where I was supposed to be
even when the sun leaves
it doesn't mean that the light has died or gone
it's just going to light up the somewhere else
where other people come from

and I learned I cannot draw a straight line under things
even when I'm calculating fractions
I drew her below the line and
me above it, always yearning for an
answer to equalise the sum of it
I spent wet break sat on the dusty gym mats with inky fingers
the colour of the tips of the wings of an aeroplane
staring at the peppermint pool
with candied discs separating the lanes
where once a girl drowned, or so I am told
I am seven, but really I am

one thousand years old

and I'm down the wrong rabbit hole

I'm waiting for a grown-up to pick me up
but my label has fallen off my hook on the cloakroom door
psi
omicron
upsilon
so many ways to spell the thing I adore
and my quilted quartz-pink coat is blushing on the floor and

I don't yet know how to bend to my own wavelength
you can't get a good report
when loving people is your academic strength
I succeed not because of but in spite of
the punctures all over my body
indoctrinated sticky sugar glaze
that traverses the sadness of the days
the breaking of my skin has always been my surrender
it makes the pain go away

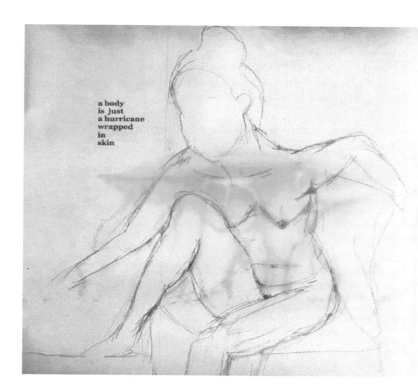

a body
is just
a hurricane
wrapped
in
skin

WEATHER: a death poem

When I am old and I die, please don't tie flowers to my coffin. Find a way to pin down forked lightning and wrap it around the wood, put a hurricane inside the case, and rest it on the Northern Lights.

Do not bury my sky inside your earth. Please don't have those flowers that spell out SISTER or DAUGHTER or WIFE – as though I was only defined by what I was to others, instead of what I am to myself. Read about physics and energy and matter at my funeral, and know that I am not in heaven because, even though I wish I was, there's such a profound difference between what you wish for and what you believe. So think of me when the streetlights pop their sodium mouths at the sky, when the darkness has such a deep pitch to it that its atoms taste like velvet in your mouth, think of me when you are lost – because if love exists for something, then it is to make us traverse the idea of the body as a destination to arrive at, and more like a place to come home to.

And when I die, don't think of me fondly. I hope there has not been one day of my life when I have evoked fondness. Never think of me with mildness, only wildness: tangles and lips and limbs and planets and tidal waves and thunderstorms – and wildness. Always wildness. Remember me as the girl who made darkness taste like a miracle.

Tie the weather to my grave. And leave the flowers for the living.

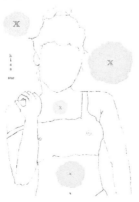

you

love me through a filter

EVOLUTION: a social media poem

I went through a phase of doing things on Facebook
so that my ex could see that I was having fun
living life for an imagined reaction
of someone who used to make me feel like the sun
is the most messed-up thing I've ever done
but I don't think that it is possible these days
to enjoy doing anything without being seen
the kids I teach take selfies of themselves doing normal stuff
like buying a bus ticket and drinking a cup of tea
because nothing counts these days any more
unless you're saying 'look at me'
unless you are turning the mundane into celebrity
unless you're creating distance between imagined pixels
and what you wish was your reality

and now people write online that their dad has died
people click like and then write
'RIP hunny [insert emoji that looks sad]'
my dad has carried me on his shoulders for thirty-three years
and his hand makes mine feel like lightning wrapped in skin
and our eyes are both green with bits of orange in
and I know I'm his best thing because he sees myself in him
and if when he dies they click like
because they don't have any kind
of adequate cognitive apparatus
I am going to let pieces of me dissolve inside
and blame myself for writing a complex human tragedy
into a simple Facebook status

and I'm sorry
but I don't want to know what you've had for your tea
but I want you to know what I've had for mine
so I'll click like so that you click like and
then we can all pretend that we are having a good time
and a good life
we're all just knocking from the inside
and this is the evolution
I'm falling in high resolution
researching lives for that dopamine hit
but this is like forensics inside a sandpit
this is a wild and ugly ride
a brutal little life

we don't talk about the things that matter
because we are all signing a petition to get class C drugs legalised
demonise the immigrants and dehumanise the refugees
and don't forget to vote Tory
change your profile to a rainbow so that
you can write yourself into someone else's oppressed gay story

and I am guilty too
if you looked at my Facebook you would think
I had the most wonderful life with the biggest smile
I'm not going to post a picture of myself when I am eating cheese

straight from the packet and watching Jeremy Kyle
if you don't like it then put a filter on it
turn up the saturation and Instagram the hurt out of it
nobody needs to know, do they?
they don't need to know that all I have done today
is feel my life dissipate and slide away
so I just post a picture from the loophole of another day
is there a difference between evolution and a miracle
or are they the same?

I look at all your highlights
that are plastered all over your wall
and I know that there's a reason that I put you on a pedestal
still I won't let you go
I want to contain you in a diode
get closer to you through hacking and cheat codes
I'm done with taking the hard road
light the way for me instead with the internet as my painkiller
framed with filters and with benzos

and lately there is too much discrepancy between my real life
and what I post about online
I have forgotten how to be joyful about the things that are mine
where someone hasn't clicked like
I miss being bored
like when you are a kid and you play games
like how many times you can flip the tab on a Coke can
and how long you can hold your breath for
and who can see ten green cars first on the motorway
(I can)
like having nothing to do
makes you do things you wouldn't normally do
and I'd lick my cuts because my blood tasted good
like a coin metallic and true
and count how many seconds I could sit next to that girl
before she moved
and I'd think about letting the green man
out from the traffic lights and setting him free
I would take my remote control around the house

so that it could be happy
I didn't want it to only know one place for its whole life
and to never see
the world apart from through a TV screen

and I guess I am still bored
but I am bored by other people
and maybe I just miss being bored of my own doing
and of my own self and my own skin
maybe I miss knowing the map of my insides
like it was an atlas of stars and planets I could grow old in
maybe I miss being me
and in my body there is no evolution
because I am too busy looking at what all of you are doing
and yet still I do not leave
I do not grow
I do not stop going online even though I know it's wrong
and all my get up and go has just
well
got up and gone

now I only do things so they look good online
I go to a museum and post a picture of a picture
and wait for people to click like
so that my need to explore myself artistically is abated
I need people to know I'm pursuing culture
to make me feel validated

and if there's no likes?
then maybe I think that museums and art aren't for me
I don't know how to make my own happiness
a private pursuit for me
so I go to bed and cry myself to sleep
but not before I check in first
it's easier to tag myself in bed
than it is to tell people
the monsters have crawled out into my head

and when I die people will say
'her Facebook presence was such an homage'

and they won't know it was a lie and a fake and a mirage
that I was friends with you even though
we had nothing in common and we disagree politically
but when we were fifteen you made me laugh
and your mum always made me my best tea
and for that I will remember you fondly with no remnant of
logic
my mind is governed by emotions
and it leans towards the nostalgic
I don't know you any more
and you don't know me
but you remind me of being home and feeling safe
and that means that I can't cut you out, you see
and all of a sudden I'm friends with people for what they were
not for who they are
and I'm about as far from happiness as I could ever be
until you click like and I feel your love coming back to me
until you click so I can be free
my life is a capitalist tragedy of throwback Thursdays
and flashback Fridays and happy humpdays
I'm just lost, looking for a way to tell you that I'm lonely
I'm trying to tell you that I've lost my gravity
and it's so much easier to lose myself in loving someone else
taking a holiday in all of your skin
that's why I love other people
because I live my life through them instead of living from within

I don't know how to form into a better version of myself
and I don't know how to improve
I'm the curator of a gallery of my life that's the opposite of truth
and I post these pictures and I write these statuses
to create distance from the fact
that all I ever really do
is think about is you
you
all I ever really do
is think about
you
you
you

there
in
only
ever
one
notification
that
we
wait for:

and i
wait
for
you

♡ 1

NIGHT DREAM: a beautiful poem

I used to sleep in my ballet shoes
in a pillow of spotlit hues and glitter net
every night I danced Odette
clinging to your feline heart in my bed
the limelight all on the satin swan of me

I refused to dream in tragedies
so I took the curtains down myself before the final scene
and I was never the witness but always the seen thing
and looked for you in every audience meeting
because I know you would consider me a thing worth seeing
we would never set foot where the goodness goes missing
we would be safe up on the stage

with the applause all ours to take
and you would hold me as people threw flowers
into our gleaming and fake
perfect mirror Swan Lake

when I was a baby my mama pressed my hands
into the handprints of Marilyn Monroe
I went back when I was eleven
to the place where all the tourists go
my hand span bigger than hers was all that time ago
I was already spilling over the shapes of the great
too big to fit on the pavement slate
most people write to forget their smallness
I write to remember it
because if you are large like me
then it's much harder to show vulnerability
because my body won't do the talking for me

I used to pull out my milk teeth
and wait for the visit from the fairy
that would give me advice
on how I could become the special sugarplum one
I used to think my toys talked about me
every time I came back from holiday
I would creep back up the stairs
in the hope to catch them having fun without me

and until I was twelve years old
I wondered why even with three blankets on
my dolly was still cold
I didn't even need a toy to move back then to believe
just enough support around me
to recognise there was even a potential for magic available to me

I never ran in kiss chase because I wanted to be caught
because if you're really in love
then it makes you betray even your own rules
most people hunt to find their prize, but I
I hunt to become the hunted

hunted is child's code for being wanted
I look for the chance
to be found over and over again

and all the older kids at school
used to say I was mad for being caught
but I was just sad and hadn't yet been taught
the difference
and since then I've been called worse by better
but I boxed my pain neatly into lines and letters
so really I should find the bullies and say
thank you
because of being hated
I now know what I value

I always was so desperate to fit in
and yet so reluctant to be ordinary
wanted to be safe but also the anomaly
I had to go on a saline drip once and I imagined
they were recharging me like a mobile phone battery
except I was a mermaid and they were filling me up with the sea
I contain all the oceans and forests inside me

if I try really hard I can hear my toys talk and the trees too
they are telling me to be brave
they are the surfaces that contain and hold my projections
in my serrated silver baby lake
I'm torn, longing for the unreal to become the real to us
to make people love me more
through the power of my telekinesis
but the trees and the toys have made their excuses
and bowed out
and the way I see light is the same as how you see time
we're both running out
and I am centre stage where the unspeakable is scripted
and therefore allowed to be spoken
and I know from far above swans' necks look like question
marks
yearning to be broken

I would never dare hurt a living thing
and yet here I am
hurting myself and waiting
to be saved by an overture and a come-to-life toy

an absence of pain is not the same
as the presence of joy

your perception of me
is just a reflection
of the gaps
you ache to fill

BIRDS: a sadness poem

they take your things away from you
at first it's horrible, but later it feels good
to have boundaries made for you
because I'm spilling over the lines
I need a grown-up equivalent of a bedtime

so I like the fire exit on the door
these are the institutional safety signs
they make me remember life is a thing
worth waiting up for

even if there's nowhere to run
outside or inside makes no difference to me
I'm trapped in this atlas
playing hide and seek with my tongue
I rip holes in the map
my exit wound coming undone
I carve circles around an escape route sun

they tell me here you get monitored in the shower
they call it suicide watch
the alarm they press sounds like
a prairie siren
it feels like someone is keeping you safe
from the deep end every hour
it feels like God
pitched in a soprano tone

suddenly I understand religion
it must be like always being under the loving eye of
a woman who loves you
unconditionally
imagine that
someone watching your every move
and being a loving guardian to your tantrums
and to your ordinary
life

I went away last summer and it was so hot that even dust stuck to my skin and then one day in the complex it rained so hard that it knocked the pink tiles off the motel swimming pool and they floated like bubblegum bruises on an upside-down kerosene sky and I sat outside in all that rain and I was happy because to have one cold day amongst all the red sun days

felt like a break in the algorithm
it felt like
a valediction

I wish you could douse memories
in gasoline
I've enough in my brain to start
a forest fire and I yearn for drought

the whole world is wrapped inside me
with the sadness spilling out

I hate that my hospital room has a plant
I know what it is like to have to root
yourself in plastic with all that
wildness contained
in artificial arms

I'm spilling out
and I dream in circuit boards
and I take my medication every night
the rush I get from being obedient
is quicker than the wait to win the fight
I am a good girl
my heart is made of burned honey

spilling

the birds will sing outside the locked doors of the wards
they will flock to the holes I make

out

in this paper world
where I can't remember
if what is real is as important
as what is true

they are not the same

my life is more than just mine

suffering has lit me

all this sadness
it undoes your living

this is a disorder

it is not a
decision

I have been busy
planting my universe
in other people's gardens-
wildflowers
look so much more
beautiful
when they bloom
in any hand
but mine

are
all
of
the
colour
baby
girl

light
me
up
like
a
whole
sunrise

BLOSSOM: A DARKNESS POEM

there's blossom in the garden and my heart is going under
I am nine and crushing catkins and lilac
in a small cracked tumbler
I am making perfume to put on the insides of my wrists
I want the older girl next door to hold me on her lap like a wish
and I can't think
of any other way to be noticed than this

my limbs are like pink liquorice

they are as sturdy as my dolly's cot
my heart is the stone of an apricot
it is a crooked thing already and bends only
towards the side she is on

I hold my hands on the kettle as it boils
soft scald on a conglomerate of flesh
the perfume will make me a martyr
I'm creating stigmata
with my skin undressing
this perfume is my love but on the outside
my fevered honey blessing

I wait for it to cool by drawing around my body with my chalks
I am not allowed outside the crime scene lines I'm making

how much compassion there is in boundaries
how much passion there is in the breaking

I bow out on the fresh-cut lawn with stripes mown out
I put my lips to the bowl to taste and to see if it shouts and
I'm paying knee-to-lip benediction with my mouth
in a body that is less cathedral

more slaughterhouse

children have such dangerous hearts

ever since I realised I could make thoughts
I knew there were rocks in my diaphragm
I learned the hard way
that when you are humiliated
it's the act of someone giving you their shame
it takes the ownership of all their bad things away
and gives it to you to hold instead

and when I told a teacher she said
that sometimes life gives you lemons
but I didn't understand that at all
on the way home I bought a bag of lemons
and sat and looked at them
and I wished life had given them to me
life hadn't given me anything at all

no girl had given me anything at all
not
yet

the perfume cools under the apple tree
I pour it in my hair and knock on her door
praying *notice me* in my head
but
n o o n e is h o m e
so I
r u n to t h e s h e d

inside the old tennis rackets there are spider eggs

I heave in the vacuum-packed air
see the neon lime bubble of the spirit level
softly watching me there
all this hot sun trapped in the tarpaulin
I press between my legs and it's her name I'm calling

later I sleep with a depth I didn't know was at the bottom of me
I'm on top of the duvet
and I'm undressed and wet and freezing cold
I am ten years old
I am ten years old

I squeeze my eyelids shut and pray
the burns feel like an analgesic
the napalm balm of yesterday

the pain is so bad that
the whites of my eyes roll back

one lap
one lap
could never be
e n o u g h
for me

I am thirty-three
I've climbed into so many
and still the flowers burn
I find no absolutions
the scripture is just kindling to
me

when I was fifteen years old
I knocked on the door again with peonies
my twin's aftershave on my skin

home tastes like
sin
we kissed and she pinned my arms down tightly
and left urgent blotches branded on my skin
broderie anglaise
there were Magic Marker lines on me that lasted for days
in the end you only really end up
with the things you give away

she tasted like catkins and lilac
she tasted like the corner of my pillow
of sweetness and violence

Mary Magdalene is still of no comfort to me
religion is just looking at the sky because we are lonely
I think we are just searching for ourselves in each other
this was the summer where I realised that idols were just statues
not a replacement for a mother

my body is a slaughterhouse
my heart is howling in the glow

I can't seem to find the Holy Ghost
and I want to talk to you
but there's such a very narrow line
between
not wanting to tell you
and desperately needing you to know

ASTRONAUT: a growth poem

when I was younger I wanted to be an astronaut
and step across Jupiter's carcass
I didn't know that the closest feeling I would get
to cosmic space helmet darkness
would be me being anxious at a gig or a party
looking into the mouths of my friends
that space bubble darkness between me and them

I cannot form the words to say that I don't belong here
with the drugged-up and famous
I used to be different
I wanted to be a zookeeper and surround myself with cages

so that the wild things in life would feel less dangerous
I wanted to be a marine biologist and see what it was like to be
held by the eight arms of an octopus and to be embraced
submerged for ages
I wanted to be an author and create a fiction
far better than my body could ever form
outside the safety of its pages

I didn't want to be this anxious girl in a dark Dalston disco
with the lights turned down low to hide the fact
that we always just wanted
to get up and go
I don't have an excuse
I just needed to go

home

you see
recently I forgot that a flower without water is still something
people forget that
leaving doesn't mean disappearing
it is just a change in form
a retreating back into the earth
and let me tell you
in the right seasons sometimes I grow so tall
that even when I vanish I leave a shadow of where I stood
so you couldn't forget me even if you thought you could
where I took up all that space was just a memory in the ground
where I saved the rocks from being
scorched by the sun

make sure you tell that to everyone
when I walk out that door
that I disappear sometimes so that I can come back next time
larger than I was
before

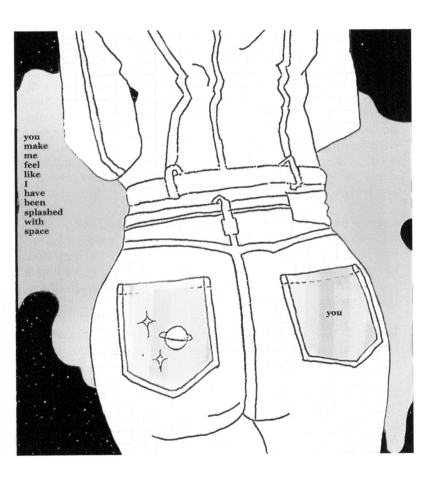

BLOOM: a support poem

Here is what to do if you have a friend who is suicidal.

Call them. Don't expect them to pick up. Leave them voicemails saying, 'No need to call me back – just saying hey.' Go to their house and tidy it, because when you're that bad it can be difficult to do basic things like stock the fridge or remember to put the rubbish out. Wash their hair with apple-scented shampoo, lean them gently over the bath and wash it and dry it for them, because it's very hard to wash your hair when things ache from your insides and apples smell like new beginnings. If you really love them – brush it out too, and dry it so it's like a halo around their head and they can feel like an angel, even if it's just for a second. Don't worry if they cannot thank you. The burden of receivership is sometimes heavy. That is not because of who you are. It is because of how things are.

Change their sheets. Depression leaves you bedbound for weeks and remains crushed between the pillows – it smells of sleep and metal. Put drinks that have fruit in them next to their bed. Leave those bendy straws, because sometimes lifting the cup is too much. Don't be scared of their anger. Anger is just sadness but in a warmer colour.

Wait with them in the emergency room. Buy them a three-year-out-of-date chocolate bar from the vending machine and be their voice when they are patronised by staff. Rub their back and wrap your scarf around them. Slide your hand inside theirs. Buy them flowers. Pretend to come to visit the flowers every day as a way to make them feel less pressured to entertain you. When they ask you why, say, 'What is the reason for a room full of flowers if I cannot see them bloom?' Hopefully they will see the metaphor. When the flowers die, remind them that even after death, the flower bed still remembers the exact way a seed needs to be cradled in order for it to grow all over again.

Hope does not vanish.
It is not gone.

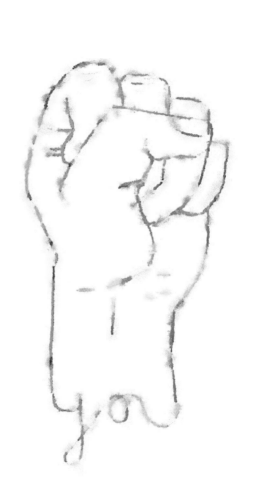

GEMSTONE: a feminist poem

I grew up with fairy tales and legends behind my eyelids
they were my collateral for a life spent hiding from the other
kids
in the cupboards at school
heart hammering in my throat
hands clenched around a sequin that's charged with static
my brain translating it into something
less like card and more like magic
a gemstone that would turn me into somebody different within
or at least give me the power to step
out of my
skin
out of my seams
I tried to step inside other people's dreams
tried to use their sweetness to fight my wrongness
I would lie awake at night
trying to press myself into their subconscious
someone told me once that if you don't dream
it means someone is dreaming of you instead
but I dreamed every night
and so I always woke up lonely
because I knew I hadn't been in someone's head

back then there were no stories about girls who saved themselves
in my head I imagined myself as a boy
rescuing the girl version of me
I read the stories of Venus and Aphrodite
but I didn't have beauty
I only had brains
and I carried Medusa in my veins
I knew that there was a better life for me than all of this
but the only god who changed their life by being bright
was Artemis
and I couldn't find a girl version of myself
apart from Helen of Troy
even she needed a costume just to break down the empire gates

I am so sick of disguises
I am so sick of being a horizon where the men's sun rises
I am so sick of my femininity being synonymous
with the word *goodness* and how it stays intact
Medusa was a good person until she was hurt
and everybody seems to ignore that fact
(Athena was angry that Medusa had been 'defiled'
so she gave her snakes for hair and wings on her back
and a stare that would turn men to stone and eyes of black
so no man would ever touch her again
but not because she was keeping her safe
but because she was jealous
and when Medusa was finally slain
out flew Pegasus)
Medusa was screwed over by men even in death
(sometimes when the boys get too close
I can smell snakes on their breath)

why don't we get taught this in school?
I was in love with my teacher and she told me
that you should become the thing you needed
and I didn't know what to be at all
and I knew this was going to be hard because I needed a miracle
I wanted my body to be more cosmic
less corporeal and

I wished that just once I could live inside a book
and I could change things from the root and the binding
so that I could change the narrative and make the storytelling
something powerful and blinding
I'll offer the mad hatter a comforting hand
I'm grown-up Alice in Wonderland
and I'm Wendy Darling in Never Never Land
I'm in love with Peter Pan
a boy who stayed alive in a grown-up world
the only difference is that my lost boy
is a girl

I'd break into *Matilda* and get her to use up her powers
to find a way to bend the light and the hours
so that I could become someone different
charming and funny
someone who could kiss and bite the lips of Miss Honey
in the bitter Dahl dark

I'd be Joan of Arc
and I would lead all the characters away from the mountain
and get out of the lake
all the while remembering that heroes with vaginas
get burned at the stake

gemstones can't magic you out of cupboards
and God knows as a woman I've been locked in all my life
I learned that there's no such thing as special freedom
but how I wish I could
take the covers off the books and make flames from this friction
to make my life a better story
than a man's perspective
on fiction
and I will
go to a museum
ask myself the question when I look at 'the greats'
with the lights down low
where are the female artists before Frida Kahlo?
where did they all go?

feminism is grief with nowhere to go

I carry in me centuries of oppression
all these fairy tales and legends
with the perspective on it all never quite right
how wide the sky
how small

our night

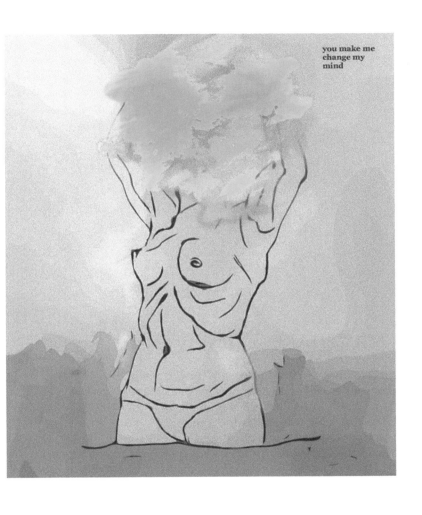

you make me
change my
mind

MILKSHAKE: an anxiety poem

I think we met inside a dream the other night
one where I owned a diner that sold pink milkshakes
and in the deep fryer there were flies
there were smashed tiles for countertops
and you had cuts on your thighs
over the plates and waitress's roller skates I saw your eyes
brighter than fireflies fucking in the tight wet nights of July

my bones

calcified

you opened your mouth and said

'one day I'm going to shut myself in a garage
and turn the gas up high and then call
and wait to be rescued just so I know what it feels like
to be pitied instead of despised
you're gonna make them notice me
my sweet little slice of apple pie'

and you knocked over the milkshake machine
and the bottles cried
soda cream tears mixed with salt from the fries

you made me think of that phrase
where they talk about a bull in a china shop
but nobody ever talks about the china shop inside the bull
I gave you all the food we had in the whole entire place
but you still didn't stop
and you still weren't full

you told me you die inside life and live inside your nightmares
so really you had met me in the best of your places
then you pulled off your face to reveal all the faces
of those who had been cruel to me and
I looked down and there were flies crawling under my skin and
out of me
muscles atrophied
I woke reaching and retching
hands in between my legs
pushing and stretching my thighs apart
I wake up every day checking the barometer of my heart
I have no idea what weather is coming
and most days it changes
but there is no man in the television warning me
when the tectonics will shift
when the storm will lift

this pain is not an aberration
and I won't give up without a fight
and I won't give up on losing you
but what I wouldn't give for a life not doomed
to be with you

even when I am without you

they tell me that you are make-believe
but I say living with anxiety is like lying in the mouth of the fire
from the belly of the beast
I will not retreat

today I dreamed about serving you food
for the 3,849th time
we made love on the finish line
in the sunlight
we rose to the gas oven of the night
I fed you pink milkshakes
which you drank with a straw from my throat
the clouds were swollen seas and my organs paper boats

I'm sorry
my dreams are absurd
we used our safe word

we died warm
we called it a lifetime
we went to paradise

there were no
more
flies

CABLE: a home poem

people are houses
others are hotels
some are both on different days
are you a place that people visit?
or are you a place where they decide to stay?

you are the dry rot and the dark spots
you are the vase full of forget-me-nots to remind me
that even though I try not to remember that you are gone
time has not forgotten you

and my ex is the bowl of keys at the door
nobody knows quite what they're for
but you keep them safe anyway just in case there is a time
when you will need to be reminded what loss tastes like again
a bit like that drawer full of things like drawing pins
and the lid of a pen
that ran out years ago
but that exact shade of red reminds you of when you were ten

my therapist
she is the bath
gleaming taps that freeze and burn
ice and warmth pouring down the plug into a single point of dark
and she will hold me just enough
to teach me how to heal as a daughter
just enough so I can learn to keep my head
above the tidemark of the water
but just enough to remind me that if I do not support myself
then the world will swallow me whole
and that will be nobody's responsibility but my own
I want to ask her every week
what is the point of a home
if I don't understand how to turn the lights on?

I want her to read me a bedtime story

where she changes the ending so that she comes to rescue me
I don't want to take accountability
I just want her to carry me like a baby

and I am scared to learn to swim in case she thinks
I can then live my life without her being in it

and my partner is completely and absolutely a room with a bed
she is softness expanding and holding where dreams are spread
the vein and the cord keeping me anchored when I hit the walls
of my dark and cracked little heart

that heart that is the cable that she cradles
as I trip over on the landing
the heart that she loves despite it being the place
hurricanes plan both their launch and their landing

loving her makes me feel like a contradiction
new and old all at the same time
like when you read the same lines in the book
but this time you are older
so they take on a different meaning
because you have become someone bolder
than the person who read them the first time around
but still
there is nothing like the sound of lying in your bed
with the rain outside the window
dreaming of sleep with the bulbs dimmed low
the glow of her body thrumming like a lantern
dreaming of sleep

my papa is the garden
vines and branches grow amongst the jungle leaves
botanic and labelled with all the questions from the in-between
and my twin is the clock
reason and hands keeping the hours safe for me
the nursery of plastic stars on the ceiling
the cosmos contained and laid out in a template neatly
and my mama is the stove and the fire and the buttons

pointing to the place where you will find the very thing
that will either save you from yearning
or at least teach you how to fall in love with the burning
my baby brother is the nail through the wood
you couldn't stay upright without him
even if you thought you could

I think that maybe my grandmother is all those things in the attic
that throb and hum above your head
that you can't throw away
because even though they're not for every day
they remind you of the person you used to be and
they hold all the parts safe that you are scared you have forgotten

but whether it was the first time
that someone touched you with intent
or whether it is your first ballet shoes
or your last school test
or a train ticket that is broken and bent
from that time you were held on a cold day
in November back in 2002
these things are here to help you
remember

I am afraid when they cut me open
all they will see is that I have always been a lie, and they
will see no kingdom nor city nor aching spark
but a motorway service station
a multi-storey car park
I bleed tarmac and dark
I'm an airport and a hospital and my cells are a queue
I'm just trying to tell you
that I'm a place that people visit
not where they stay

people are homes
others are hotels

some are both on different days
are you a place that people visit?
or are you a place where they want to stay?

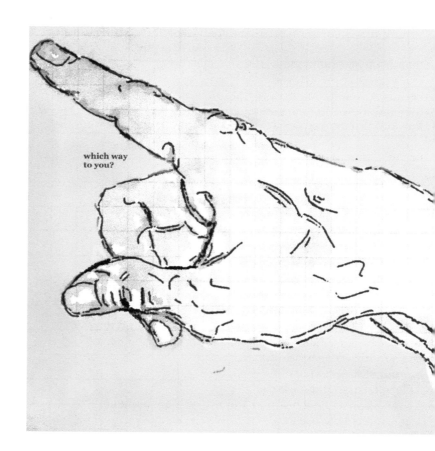

which way
to you?

SKYPHONE: an endurance poem

I wake up before the colour
eyes burned from my phone
being alone tastes like acetone
it makes me check my horoscope
even though I don't believe
I read about what I should or could do
the star signs are my only clues to you
I rely on the stars to keep my need abated
(but you cannot phone the sky and so I am never sated)

my anxiety sleeps evenly
parallel and spooned
and as she does I research
how many women have been on the moon
I imagine them pressing down into my head and
I am waxing crescent in my bed
I am everywhere else but here
and
you should see the places I go with you
when I wash the dishes at night
when I pull up the bedsheets tight
the places that we travel
boundaries ground into the gravel
echoing in the space dunes
this is the sum of them
this is our requiem

I have no idea what I am doing; I am
just a gradation of the lives before me
sometimes I feel my heart lifting
out of my ribcage to chase what could be
it's like our minds got stuck
with the same magnet from the same strip
you make me feel like closing my eyes is a lunar eclipse
and no matter how far away in the world I am
I feel myself being pulled toward you
like we were half of each other

like we weren't meant to be two but
one
you remind me I can always cross the borders
and I can always run
(but the answer to
'how many women have walked on the moon?'
is none)

a break in the mirror is a glitch
in the matrix
maybe I'm the reflection and this is a lie
and the real me lives through the glass on the other side
a break in my bone
even when healed there'll always be that fracture
our coming together will remind me always
of the day things shattered
a break in my spirit, internally gaslit and stuck in classic erosion
my brain buzzing Jackson Pollock: a lilac explosion

but the difference is this
a break in my heart
is like a
metamorphosis

this is love without
the whole of it
the fault lines on the atlas
are just drawings
to us
our bodies are merely corporeal proof
of what happened the day
the magnets met

this love is not finished
not ever
not yet

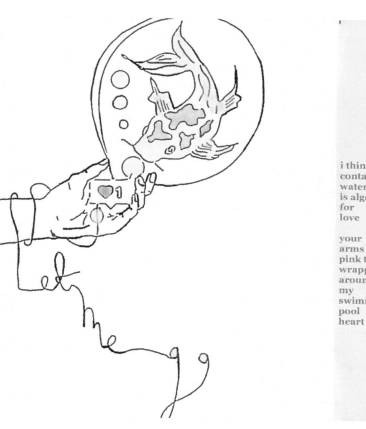

i think
containing
water
is algorithm
for
love

your
arms like
pink tiles
wrapped
around
my
swimming
pool
heart

SWIMMING: an underwater poem

when I was little
my mum called the bumps in the road sleeping policemen
early one morning
I went out with a spade and tried to crack them
I was frantic that the metal couldn't slice through the pavement
I imagined them struggling to breathe under the cement
I spent hours crying
because I knew what it felt like to be trapped as well
planning escape routes for the men in the road who slept
neatly under the asphalt swell
left out in the rain like buried landfill

every week my papa took me swimming and I let my body sink

it was the place I could be a paradox
and by that I mean
holding my breath was the only way that I knew how to be alive

by that I mean
that I was a graph looking for my coordinates

by that I mean
I was a sky looking for my constellations

I was just a person
I was looking for you in every way
the grate at the bottom of the pool
glowing like a diamond in retrograde
that black
that coal
it lit the landmines in our way

the only way for the ache to stop
was when I didn't feel landlocked
my lungs turning static in the
Kodak blue

and I can't tidy my pain away
so drowning it was the best thing I could do

now I am older my body sings when it is submerged
being with you is like
diving underwater and the
blue is impossible and the blue
it surrounds me
and the chlorine burns my eyes
and bleaches me
clean

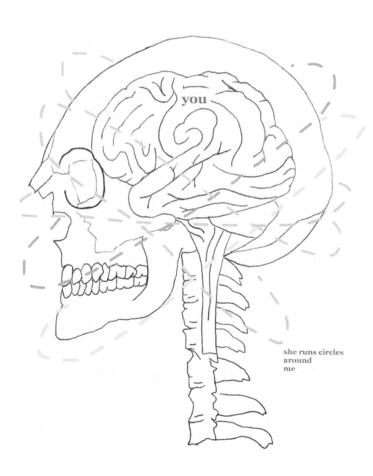

you

she runs circles
around
me

DAZZLED: a love poem for Cc

I wish that things looked the same way they felt
maybe then I would look less like a person
more like an equinox
when I opened my mouth the whole paradigm would shift
you'd remember your ribs
and be grateful for them being the only thing holding in
your sugar-spun star glum
bubblegum eclipse of a
heart

I call you my little prince

private names are my witness
I'm so full of love I can't turn down my muchness
I can be a hard woman to adore
my organs are in uproar
my fingers leave you astral dipped
lollypop licked, hat tricked and star gripped
I'm tracing Orion on your fault lines
this is a braille for only you
and
I

I won't stop calling out until the neighbours know your name
my love puts sound to shame
I make them lean to your side so much they get whiplash
my love is a chronic supersonic swimming pool splash

it makes them relive every mistake
it reminds them they're awake

and I make them wonder if they want you too
they press their walls and imagine they are close to you
they dream of their lives if they had been with you
they'd change their hair and paint their rooms
the exact shade of sky that's spliced in your eyes
lapis lazuli

they would rename
the colour blue to be called the colour
you

that's how much I love you

I'm your ride-or-die and I'm loud and strange
when I love you there's climate change
it's Malibu and juice tipping all over the plastic
tripping all over the light fantastic
glitter scorched into my moan
your name inside every single groan
you make me feel like pain
is less like paper and more like flame

I'm bending to you in every way

and when people tell me
that I love too hard and that I'm too much
I tell them that perhaps it's them who are not
enough
and I make them ashamed of all the things they did not say
and the words they didn't do
I make them remember what the words 'I miss you' feel like
when they are expressed
instead of held in their mind
I could undress
you for a thousand lifetimes
a million days
and still be
amazed
because of you I see in prisms
I am under your spotlight
and I
am
dazzled

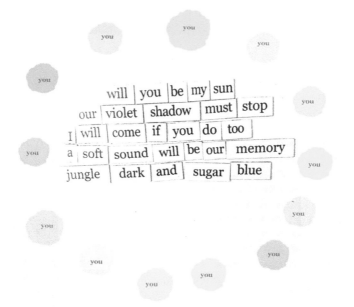

LITMUS: a mental health poem

I have been looking on the internet to
move to places where perhaps I could become
someone who doesn't live in her head
I wonder if my skin would sing differently instead
if the ceiling within and above me
had not yet seen
the alphabet of days I spend in bed
if it had not seen
me wake up in the blue hour calling out
the atoms in the air cradling my jaw
moving my mouth into the shape
of your name
I plead for sleep to take me back
to the only place where I can hold you again
in my dreams I am with you and I am
home

I know that if I were to leave here I would feel like a spectre
a shadow of our letters would sing sideways in my solar plexus
this room has seen our life and how it is glowing and violent
I have called out your name in every light
right down to ultraviolet
but now we have to go instead
and my longing is infrared
the next tenant will call our names out in his bed
that he didn't even know he knew
he will have your name on his lips
he will absorb the energy of me
and you

I just want to live in a place I can call my own
where there isn't blackness in the wood
I am so tired of cleaning away the dirt of strangers
again and again
where the shadows of different lives leave their mark
there's not a single shade of paint that can hide that
darkness

not even bleach and its alkaline kiss
I spell out letters for you in the tiles of the fridge

this is my declaration of love
this is the only way that I know how to speak to your memory
this is a nod to the litmus of language
the grammar
of grief

this is not a household
this is not a house that is held
it rages under the saltwater sun
it bruises where the curtains come
undone

I don't know where to put my body
when there is all this world to see
and yet there is nowhere left
to run

sometimes depression makes my brain leave my body

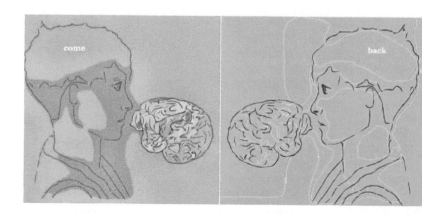

LORD'S PRAYER: a school poem

when I was learning PE
it would have helped
if they had made us stand facing one another
and tell each other one thing that made us beautiful
even though some of us could not run
life for some
is not a competition and it is not a race
some people don't have tanned legs
or a high ponytail or a beautiful face
some people like me
have legs so white that they glow blue and violet
some people halfway through cross-country gather up lilacs
and press the flowers' beauty so firmly into themselves
they leave marks on their knees
after all, there is no point in people racing
if there are not others standing carefully
waiting
to watch them bloom

physics could have been a place to explore philosophy
and the sonic boom
a place to discuss our sonar resonance
and our place in the solar order of things
biology could have been about veins and the nervous system
and why our bodies sometimes destroy themselves from within

Father, I was cut out the wrong shape for school
for all this
a life that has left me dangling on the precipice
why didn't we talk in chemistry about how to emulate bliss
about the chemical reaction of a cosmic kiss
so I could sit with her and find an explanation as to why
whenever her lips touch me
my spine sings
and I feel like I'm in heaven and I've swallowed the sea

see, why didn't we talk in english
about how to use words to replace our fists?
we should have been given a choice
why didn't you teach us the grammar of our feelings
and the meaning inside our reasons
and how to carve our own kingdom?
in RE why didn't they tell me how hope could be curated
that people could be cathedrals and bodies could be sacred
that I would find my religion
and that it is just a word that really means
believe

they kept on asking me what I wanted to be
and I knew my safe answer
lawyer
one kid
married
take my daily bread
I couldn't tell them that I wanted to be a lightbulb
and an astronaut and a poet
because there wasn't a form for these thoughts inside my head
no clear-cut career trajectory
but there isn't a formula for how to be happy
so I stuck to my story and my family of three
(and thought of taking a lover
with those lilacs pressing shapes in my knees)

in maths they should have told me how to calculate the weight
and the heaviness that loving her leaves on my skin
and the exact angle a hand needs to be placed
on the small of my back
for me to feel comfort within
geography should have been about the difference
between an immigrant and a refugee
so I didn't have to find out for myself
why the possibility of drowning in an ocean is preferable
to the probability of burning on the earth
why didn't you teach me that sometimes the body
can make its own emergency safe place

a home with eyes for windows and brains for attics
and hearts for fires burning in the hearth?
how could I learn to release the sky from its duty
of being such a very large thing?
I wanted to hold it tight to my chest
blue for the mothering

aged fifteen I loved drama
because it taught me that the pain I felt inside
could fuel something bigger than sadness
and even though I was bad at art
the chaos felt better in a lithograph
than it did in my head
I couldn't draw fruit in a bowl and use the correct shading
but I knew pain
and I did my best to make the shapes into something intelligible
and more beautiful than my hands were capable of conveying

wrapped in tea towels and sheets
I could feel the burning next to me
chest bound and tied down in surrendered androgyny
I was the angel and she was the king in the Christmas nativity
as I forgave the pain that trespassed in me
poems made sense of what I couldn't unsee

every assembly I would roll down my skirt
and scuff my shoes against the wooden flooring
listen to the morning drawing in and speak the Lord's Prayer
move my mouth so it would sound the same
think about the hallowed darkness in our chests instead
the tip of my tongue on the roof of my gums
calling out your name even though
I didn't know it yet
still
I knew your shape because it was the exact fit
for the parts inside me that were
missing

HOLIDAY: a longing poem

we were a relationship built entirely
over cable lines and phones and
I lived in a townhouse and only felt grounded
if I did things in opposites
for this reason, if I spoke to you
which was very rare
I made sure that I did so at the very top of the stairs
putting my feet through the gaps in the bannisters
and making them
dance through the slices of sun in the air

you described your house to me
you said it was a Georgian build
I knew you sat next to a Victorian lampshade and you
said you
had seen enough to make your heart enter into its middle ages
even though you were not yet
thirty
you said there was no water that could clean his hands away
so you always felt dirty
I didn't listen properly
I have always had a habit
of making holidays out of people
and I was busy
using you as a fire escape
from a life I did not know how to maintain
I suffered loneliness because I made you
both my escape and my home
my suburban happy ending
and a dangerous walk out on my own
that is a paradox that is impossible to contain too
that way I made the unobtainable out of me and out of you
you became the weather outside
but you were the blanket holding me too
I started seeing you at the bottom of my cup of tea
you stained the ceramics
and my hands couldn't reach the bottom of the mug

to clean your face away
and my fingers started to feel like they were made out of rust
yellow and orange
and bruised with a longing that turned good things
to dust

I didn't know a chest could blush
under a devised meeting of you at the doorway
how violent the body
physically reacting to the make-believe in your head

what I want to know is this
where does the adrenaline go when there is no face to kiss?
I don't know a lot
I know you can't measure grief on
a phone line
I know that you can construct texts that are responses
to conversations that you wish had happened
but never did
I know that you can't judge how long it will take
before time starts to give you the gift
of forgetting that you inhabit your skin
again
what I want to know is this
how is it possible to unlearn a love that
never
even
happened?

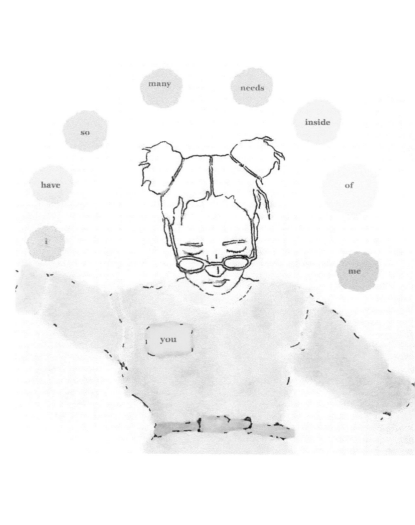

RETROGRADE: a flower poem

maybe we should wait until all the flowers die
then we could lie down over their graves
as they lay on ours
and we could pay them back for
being witness to our deaths
for all this time
I would weep at the feet of the magnolias
I would spell out their names with my limbs
MOTHER DAUGHTER LOVER
and I would lay myself down at their stems
every Sunday after church I would mourn for them
they would etch my head into the gravestones under the sky
and I would open my arms and live my life at their leaves
and give my life to making their death look
more beautiful
just because of all the things they have done for us and
all of the things they will still do
for me

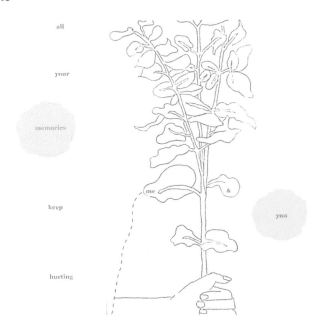

CONTACT: a bath poem

it is springtime and the light is insane
it's a 4.48 psychosis dipped in pink lemonade
a screeching Sarah Kane of a thing
the moon a drop of lactic acid with citric sting
in the twitching muscle of the sky

today I am half loud but half shy
(a contradiction and a liar)
half fraud but half messiah
half burn but half ache
I am sat in the bath eating alphabet shapes
my flesh a scalded and fizzing hot split peach
my fat a candy tropic island with a butter-yellow beach
the electric bathroom disco lights
settle their spectrums softly on my lines

in the wet dark my heart feels like a terrible bird
I bind my legs together for a makeshift tail
and I practise the word

H E

I'm thinking underwater right to the sea
imagining it is flooding all my dreams of the day
my life is my forced swimming test where I win first place
for a badge I never wanted anyway
sewn to my school blazer for no other reason than to say
that swimming is a poor substitute for being a
mermaid trapped inside Plato's cave
the fact I never told them what was going on seems so absurd
so I try the word in the dirty bathroom sea
I try the word

H E

I'm learning at psychotherapy school
that a new-born infant needs to be mirrored by an adult
to grasp that she has an outer surface

I am the same when I am overpowered
I forever looked for myself in you
there were no substitutes
but on the black days I had to look for myself in something other
I tried to make myself a mirror mother
those prisms provided me with a fragment of low relief
for a life spent not feeling seen and not being well
I try the word again but fuller this time

H E L

it is a bruise before arnica
it's a tidal swell
I promised that I wouldn't be the one to tell
I look for things that make my life sound
like a thing worth listening to
I'm framing me in carnation pink
my lens is lagoon blue
a warped and foetal diamond tilted straight toward you

I get out the x of the alphabet shapes and place
it right up at the y-axis of my face
X is such a funny word for us to miss
it's like sounding out the shape that we use for a kiss
I am beautiful and I am strange
my word could make your rivers rearrange
but still I cannot say

H E L P

submitting to you was synonymous with my deliverance
you took all the things that hurt and dipped them in limerence
you held me when the days sizzled slow-burn
traumatic dissonance
and turned them into something crackling
visceral
somatic sibilance
you're the litany to my bruises
and you made me feel less like a thing pain happened to
and more like a thing chance chooses

in my bath I am perfectly still
but it's the fastest I have ever felt
there is so much movement in the static
my stillness is the word help but coded in my own hieratic
how much energy there is in my surrender
how much I can render what happened obsolete
because asking for H E L P is so hard, you see
I was completely on my own
and now I am still a skeleton
waiting for my ghost
to come
home

the only change is that now
I'm your zeitgeist and
the need to fill the need
is bigger than the need
to get rid of it

H E L P

when I close my eyes I see
orange trees doused in dust
a silicon sunrise turning on and off
lemon groves trembling with citrine lust
syringes covered in rust
Valium packets dipped in dust

we all spend our lives longing to be loved and
yearning for the dead
and trying to make our pain make sense
so that we can work out why the world chose us
and not someone else instead

I must be tender to my own regression

I must be tender to what makes me me
but I must remember
what keeps me safe
is also what makes
me

hungry

I don't believe in signs
I just believe in noticing things
that our subconscious knew we needed
with more clarity
one day I'm going to be part of my mirror's reverie
and my eyes will dazzle
like molten coins at the bottom of the sea
and I am going to get to live my life again and make them all see
my lips when I spell out
S E E
M E

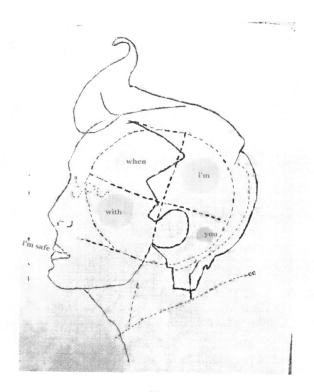

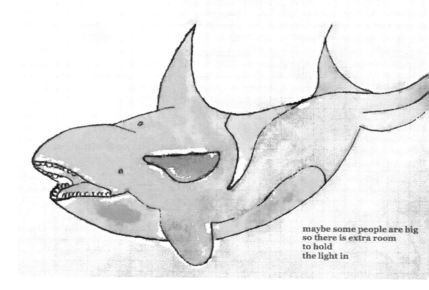

maybe some people are big
so there is extra room
to hold
the light in

TAMAGOTCHI: a diet poem

sometimes I have to pretend that I'm a Tamagotchi
so that I can see if I'm tending to my needs
I imagine I live inside the tiny pixelated screen
and there's a giant nurturing hand
controlling me
telling me what to do and checking if I have eaten
and asking if I'm okay
I don't know what to do about food and how to keep myself safe
my body on some days is my saviour and other days it is my
grave

I feel a comfort in that sometimes the fridge
is the only light that illuminates at my command
sometimes being told that I should lose weight
feels less like a reprimand
more like love
like hope

I'm paying penance with my hands down my throat and yet
there's still a weighing scale blooming at the nape of my neck
if I could I would devour the whole entire sunset
I think eating for me is like a promise ring
food keeps me safe
yet it's the thing I stay trapped in
you dream of boulevards and sunset strips
but I dream in chocolate bars and packets of crisps
salt and vinegar stars on my lips
I'm pressing my sugar paper hips and I'm
red in the spaces where the balm should be
and yet when I see my belly reach up
breaking bath water
I am Moses
parting the red
Dead Sea

what about the me that never visits the mirror
the one that doesn't need to look at itself to feel real
where is she?

I think maybe it is a myth that dying makes you whole
that death is in some way a completion
a finishing
and being full is the only time that pain feels
less like power
more like a small thing diminishing
I think I have been stuck in this consciousness for too long
and I can't grow
I think maybe I'm still bruised from another lifetime
that happened a century ago
and I cannot find a way to finish my existence
so at least when I binge
I feel in some way like I can be safe
at the edge of the chasm of things

how easily food makes me change my adult mind
about what I am

I'm a greedy girl with a hungry pulse
my cardiogram is less like neat and tidy up-and-down lines
more like a Polaroid of churros and candyfloss
full-fat cola and fast-food fries
but with safety in calories comes great sacrifice

part of me wishes I was small
so that I could curl at my therapist's feet to
beg her to stamp on me
and then feel my heart heal as I see her refuse
I was that thin once and it rendered me into a child
it made strangers maternal instead of something wild
when I was naked you could see every bone
and all of a sudden I had a thousand more mothers
who wanted to take me home

my ribs glittered like rhinestones

but now
my body makes me ashamed and it
has outgrown my pain, and now
I have to tell you
when it hurts
but sometimes I wish I could show you
if I was small I could just sit on your sofa
and say nothing for the entire time
and you'd know my heart was breaking
without me saying anything
being mentally ill is a paradox
because I want to be the one who heals
but I also want to be the one you all admire
for surviving despite the aching

I am aching for wings
desperate for ground
to be weighed down by something bigger than me
my voice calling through that Tamagotchi screen
it is pleading for the inedible
it is pleading

'love
me
please be soft with me
my body is home
to a life'

PINK: a sexuality poem

my whole life I've been told to sit with my legs closed
to check my ego
told 'you'd look nicer
if you'd let the hair over your shaved scalp grow'
hidden my pink cheeks after the older girls made me glow
been the straight girl's conquest
a taboo twist in her development
a story to tell the grandkids
an erotic experiment
a neurotic wish to tell the therapist
(a lesbian kiss was something
she always wanted to tick off her bucket list)
when I was thirteen we finally got the internet
I listened to the dialling tone with my heart in my chest
and cried when I looked up what lesbian meant
(yet I've still been told I just haven't met the right man yet)

see, I didn't play with trucks or tools
I didn't get picked first at school
for softball or dodgeball or any kind of ball at all
I picked pink over blue, so that made me a girly girl
not like the girls at school with the flat chests and curls
so when they found out –
because apparently I owed everyone a 'coming out'
because I had to make public what I deemed was my 'fate'
(I don't see anyone having to tell their parents they're straight) –
they boxed me as a femme
but I don't like dresses and I don't like lipstick
but I don't wear a tool belt, so that means I must like dick
my hair's long but it's a mess
I have tattoos on my arm and an ache in my chest
my heart is enormous and
gender is just a performance
and I have been always so very good at playing my part
I've got playing hapless femme down to an art

and my act
you bought it
don't ever tell me being gay is a choice and that you support it
I would never have chosen to be ostracised
I didn't choose how girls felt between my thighs

and people say, 'when did you first know?'
and 'who goes on top?' and 'how do you guys do it?'
as if asking me is their way of showing how cool they are with it
and I say, 'oh, I always knew it'
my first kiss was like the fire burning within me was finally lit
I craved sympathy and validation from female authority
(I wanted my prefects and teachers in bed with me)
girls, they crawled under my skin
and set up camp inside my arteries
my first kiss with my best friend
tasted like the cosmos had touched my face
aged eight in the attic, our tongues sweet after tinned pineapples
locked and shocked in a sugared embrace

so if one more straight person says to me
'wow, it must be so cool being gay'
then I'm going to ask you to stare your ninety-eight-year-old
grandmother in the face
and see how easy it is for you to tell her
'I'm not what you thought I was growing up
and I hope that that's okay'

see your friend anxiously check if you're looking at breasts
whenever a woman walks past
wondering if you've got more scratches on your bedpost
than the whole sum of woman from his past
'do you finger girls the same as him?
do you like woman with curves or woman who are thin?
woman with large tits and tight hips and dark eyes?
or don't you have a type?
do you like it to be a surprise
when you dress them down in the bedroom?
anyway, tell me soon

your sexuality not being of the norm means that you owe it to us
to make your private matters public, you see
remember you are lucky that we accept you
despite your shortcomings
so make your answer kind to me (and extra pc)
make it so that my neighbour can say
she met a lesbian at a dinner party
and she was actually quite pretty and she had quite good taste
such a terrible shame she is a lesbian, really
such a waste'

why do I have to explain away this alchemy to strangers in bars?
you don't find drunk people asking why the sky holds stars
it just does, whether or not you ask
we can split the sky apart with physics
and talk about the dreams it prohibits
and we can talk about love as chemistry and my body as biology
but sometimes there isn't a word for how my partner fills me

how can I explain
that you cannot fix something that is not broken?
that there's no need to make me the straight girls' token?
that where I am cracked is just where the light shines through?
that I'm not pink and I'm not blue
I'm just a girl in love with a girl
that should be enough for

you

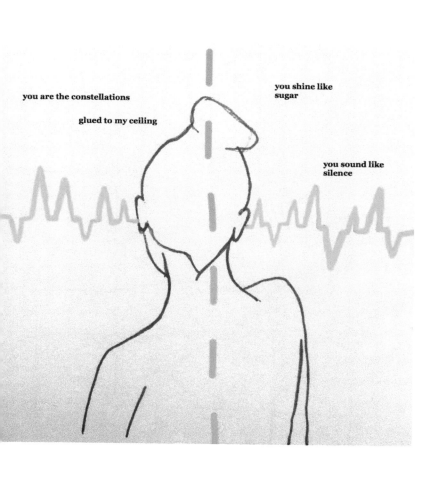

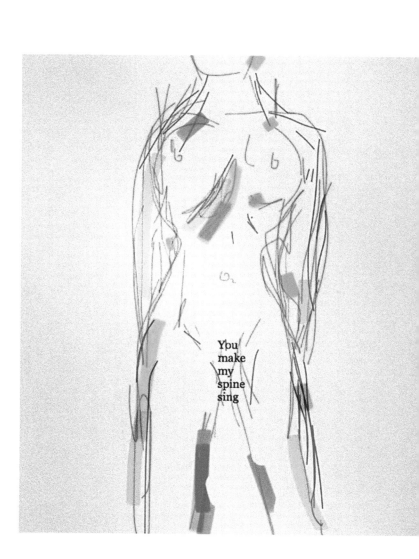

You
make
my
spine
sing

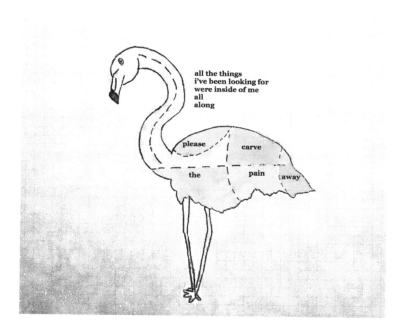

all the things
i've been looking for
were inside of me
all
along

please carve

the pain away

LAUNDRY: a maturity poem

the launderette is Listerine and Colgate green
it could be any time because the sky is in between
(everything is liminal in this
halcyon avocado dream)
Mama used to sit the baby by the cloud screen to watch this
an aquarium but with clothes for coral and plastic orbs for fish

there's always gum stuck under the vending machine
but this one is different to the one at school
instead of snacks you can pick your fabric softener out
one that is for silk especially and one that gets the stains out
the numbers are rubbed off so you have to count
the one I choose every time is number nine because I like the way
the tail of it curls in my mouth when I say it out loud
I like the memory of the way

nine feels
like having your whole life just laid out in front of you
like a cartoon
with the sound turned down
no heaving noises from the utility room
teeth not yet crowding the underside of your jaw
not a moment yet where you took
the toothbrush away from your mouth
and saw blood for the first time in the plastic hook
teeth that were white like the cartoons
before the first time you realised yours could turn yellow too

before you become more like coal broken at the baseline
less like a gold token from the deep mine
like a bad joke with an even worse punchline
that a drunk uncle forgot
a time when if you stood in the fire
it only burned away what you were
not

I still can't sleep without the blanket that used to line my cot

the clothes wrap around each other and are held
in a way that they can't be in the drawer
the tights wrap their legs around the arms of a vest
jumpers are knotted at the neck
there's always more
to the story when you realise
that even the clothes crave each other's affection
the only difference between the knot that ties the cape and noose
is the intention
I bet they are relieved to have a break
from a lifetime spent bending to my shape
I imagine tiny clothes in there as though I have the courage
to one day have a daughter
I'm falling in the daydream of no gravity in water
maybe she would be forced to absorb my trauma
she would be born bloated
with her lips wrapped around the word *no*

look, I don't know

I know that if you lick soap it tastes like salt
and when your grandmother
scrubbed the swear words out your mouth
the cold water making the roots of your gums shriek in pain
you thought you would never taste the number nine again
so soap tastes like telling him to fuck off and to come again
all in the same breath
does a troubled life make a more worthy death?
this pain has to be worth something, surely
there has to be a point to always feeling so poorly

all the while the washing machines open their whole mouths
they're not afraid of having the backs of their throats washed
out
and then they are singing under the biodegradable sky
their hymn of regret-stained soap-sud serenades
songs as an antidote for all the toxic touch
trapped and dazed in the grey days

I was only nine

where does the soap go when it's drained?
does the soap that kisses my clothes
ever meet with the soap that kisses yours too?
does the water drained from our days ever combine
so there's some way in this world I am close to you?

suddenly the dryer is a starburst and a vortex galactic
I put my finger under the rubber rind lips
bending snapping elastic
and there is black mould pixelating the mouth anaphylactic

I am drying my clothes in something dirtier
than the body that they came off
ruined before my becoming

the posterity of dust
the zealous sun
the deed is done

the streetlights spit at me and
I see myself reflected back in that vending machine
I'm burning phosphorous lemon and dirty tangerine
aurora borealis abundant on my jaw
mould in patterns on the ceiling and doors

this is my Sistine chapel
and every bedsheet comes out a masterpiece
I am Michelangelo
turn me inside-out
I was only nine
put Vanish on my heart
douse my skin in starch
life hiding through a fish's eye
make me clean of the memory of the pain

the way a story sounds
and the way a story feels
are not always
the same

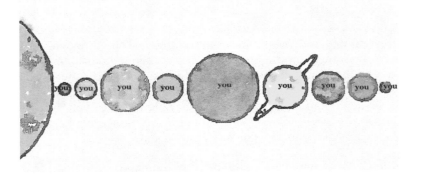

IF THE PLANETS HAD A SMELL:
a comfort poem

The moon: like a cinema when it's quiet and dark, and you have popcorn and the carpet has just been hoovered – and you haven't started your pick-and-mix yet, and you know you need to pace yourself with it but you can feel the sweets fizzing like rainbows under your fingers, and the light from the projector above you is round and pale like a milk bubble, like a soap sud, like a pear dipped in syrup.

Mercury: like something sparkling and singed – like birthday cake candles freshly blown out in an expensive room that has curtains that are so heavy that they practically shut themselves to protect a room that's shy from the gaze of the constellations, and there are ceramic vases that are coloured like the elements, in treasure pink and jungle green, which are always full of peonies that are just about to open their mouths into lavender gasps.

Venus: like when you go swimming at a water park and you come out and you smell like chlorine all day and it feels good like a secret, and your fingernails are bleached white from the pool and your stomach balances on the edge of a bottomless and ravenous hunger that can only be abated by hunks of bread drenched in butter, and you spend the rest of your day exhausted and playing with your pastel-coloured macaroon Polly Pockets and living safely inside the imagining.

Mars: like petrol and asphalt, like an outdoor court after it's been a tropical day and you sneak in to use the basketball hoops, and there are orange floodlights that turn on when it's dusk, and one day you think in your head that you'd like to live in America or somewhere really far away, and you'll be better somehow just for the act of being there, and you'll be able to scale every cactus fence and every damaged skyline because you always knew it, you always did, you are, you are a movie star.

Jupiter: like statues that are made of granite and stone that have been around for millions of years and smell of rain, and once on a school trip you touched one in a museum and your teacher shouted at you and it's your first memory of the richest emotion you have ever felt in your whole life: shame. When you are older you will think of Jupiter every day because shame is where all the good things lie. Listen to it; it tells you what matters to you, and it tells you where your boundaries are, and never to betray yourself to maintain a connection.

Saturn: like an electrical current short-circuiting – the spaces between the alphabet; like when you made a bulb in double physics and it blew up because you made it too bright and you and your friends laughed so much that you were sent out for being hysterical, and if that isn't a metaphor for life then I don't know what is.

Uranus: like inhaling brand-new tennis balls and going to Majorca and sitting quietly breathing in the inflatable dinosaurs and flamingos in the little shop at the end of the road that smells of honeysuckle, like longing, like when you are a kid and you have money to spend but nowhere to go.

Neptune: like the sea and freshly sharpened pencils and blunt crayons and salt and limes and bar codes that haven't been scanned and brand-new books that you haven't turned the corners down on yet and they all wait for you like a new body ready to get discovered just by the act of you loving them.

Pluto: like the smell of a water ride at Disneyland that's called something exotic – like Typhoon Storm or Lullaby Lagoon – and your dad holds your hand tightly on it and gets you your very own raincoat and for the millionth time you think you couldn't love him more and yet here you are, and at the end you line up and you get a little photo on a plastic glitter keyring that you keep on your schoolbag until you're too old to need a schoolbag any more and you wish you could remember where you put it and then later you find it in a box in the loft and your smile is exactly the same curve shape as your papa's and you press the glitter in the keyring and all of a sudden you are ten and asleep in the back of his car with a soft toy and the football on the radio and outside it has been dark forever and you are not even nearly home but it doesn't matter because you are with him so you are safe, you are safe, and Pluto isn't even called a planet anymore but that doesn't stop it from carrying on just as it always did, whether or not someone deemed it worthy, because in my dad's eyes no matter the names people call me I am always part of his solar system.

The sun: like a morning in the garden when there is dirt under your nails and your knees hurt and you close your eyes and you feel all the things you planted under your feet and how their roots reach and reach for each other, like hands, and it's beautiful but it's overwhelming too – all the things that grow and do not need you to be witness to them blooming in order to be extraordinary.

A star: like bottled lightning and fizzy lemon sherbets and the feeling you get when you think you have forgotten something and then you realise that you had it all along and the relief floods your bones like a homecoming – like when you throw a boomerang perfectly and it comes back to you like a dream – like flying.

RAINBOW: an LGBT poem

just as the times in the glow
when between us there are strings of silence
deep down I know
in the spectrum of things
red cannot ever lie close to violet
you talk about this rainbow never having an end
a cyclical bind of alchemy
you imagine it as a complete and obsolete bend
(no space for you left to lie next to me)

but you do not think about the things that lie either side of it
red never merges into violet
and that's just the size of it

either side of the prisms that begin and end this light
there comes that cellophane sky
a desperate aching kind of white

and so when you talk about the space the rainbow inhabits
and the patterns that it weaves
I think about the edges of the surroundings of the shapes
and the imprints that it leaves

there's five whole colours between us
orange, blue, yellow, indigo and green
and some nights I dream in monochrome
and it makes me feel weak

some nights I dream in colour
even though some days pride is a
language I cannot speak

and this flag is our emblem
the emblem of whatever someone else decided it means to be
gay
as if we needed something to make our love less like a victory
and more like a cliché

let's cover the flag in sparkles
and place it at the roof of a unicorn's mouth
because god forbid we be represented by something too complex
for some straight people to figure out
it is neat and so much easier this way
just to say
'we are friendly and cheerful and we love being gay'

as if a rainbow could represent the complexities
of how small her hand feels in mine
and I am sick of the kids asking me
'miss, why isn't there a straight pride?'
I always say
'because a march where your sexuality is represented
would be just as simple as living your life'
and so there's no sign or colour for what you do at night
because there is no need for you to convey the subtleties
of how love has eclipsed your life
supermarkets aren't making £3.99
out of putting your lifestyle on a T-shirt and calling it
PRIDE
advertisers aren't making a filter that scribbles out all of the
darkness of your life
it's like the only way that society can tolerate us
is if we glitter

but what about
if I prefer
to
glow?

and in their rainbow there is no space left for her to lie next to
me
because even though she's red and I'm violet
it doesn't change the fact that loving her
always brought out the best in me
and the way she held my ribs felt like we were making history
and around her I'm a better kind of me
the kind of person who never let the divisions
of flags and human boundaries stop me

my love for colours is just an allegory

so leave me here with her in the dark in a place where it is silent
because I know deep down
that red will never hold hands with violet
I like the edge and the taste and ache of her kiss
and the way she looked when she handed me a cigarette lit
and said

'Beth, this is it
no rainbows, no sky with stars all lit
just you and me and darkness split
don't you feel all the more beautiful
just for knowing it?'

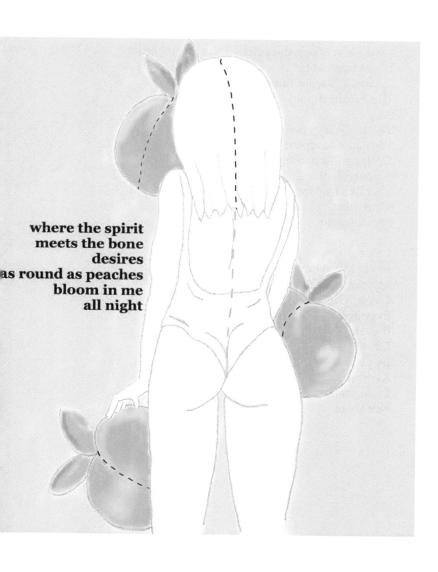

where the spirit
meets the bone
desires
as round as peaches
bloom in me
all night

SOFTNESS: a tender poem

Softness without the prick of the thorn before it
Is just normality
Contrast is what makes
The extraordinary
Sing
The long days before you
Were just blueprints
Designed to make your arrival
A concrete thing
Less like hurting
More like
Breathing in

I'm just saying you're the only girl
I ever loved enough to want to leave
My cardigan at yours
Overnight and my stomach doesn't
Even feel tight at the prospect of leaving
It curled up on your chair
I don't mind a part of me in your house
Just softly there
Reminding you I have arms to hold you
Even when I'm
Not there

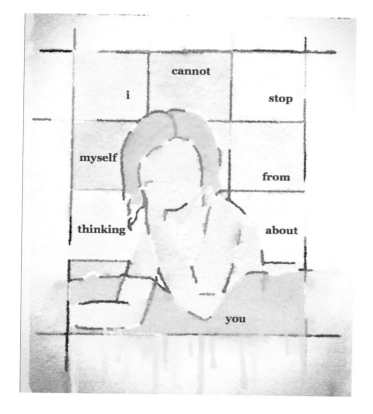

GONE: a death poem

you think I am gone
but I speak to you
every day

I have made the fruit fall for you
left feathers outside
your front door

I have turned the traffic lights
tangerine too early
just to keep you safe

and I have hidden your coat
so that you were late enough
to see the whole sky shift
pink

I made the light leave early this year to make
autumn arrive because I know how much
you love it when the leaves pour gold
over the ground

I have made your favourite song come on the radio
three magpie mornings in a row

and kept the milk tasting sweet for one whole day more
than it should have done

every night when you fall asleep
and you are crying out and your
hands drag themselves against the wall
and you call out
'please
why won't you answer me?'

listen
to the pipes creaking in the dark
to the roar of the traffic outside
it is me telling you
that as long as you are here
I
am here too

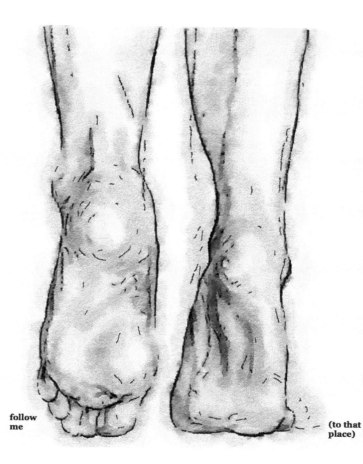

follow
me

(to that
place)

ATLAS: a betrayal poem

you had no passport because you used the
bodies of lovers as your horizons
their veins an atlas
a single cry out
volcanic and private like the quiet
architecture of two dark shapes folded

asleep like a mountain beneath my hands
you saw the sky inside my open mouth
a city laced inside our cold-sweat grasp

the opposite always seems to occur
here
just where the anti-solar point lies
the exact nucleus on the sky sphere
directly opposite where the sun shines

this love is in me

and the thing you have most in common with
is the galaxy
it too is gravitationally
bound and made of star clusters and cosmic rays
stellar remnants
an unexplored compound
of dark matter gathered up into days

the strong arms of my shadow are the plane
that propels you forward still in freeze-frame

an equinox inside a treasure chest
inside a vortex
this is truth at best

you told me you would leave me tomorrow
my body was still your world with sky lit like madness
dipped in the tropics, stunned like summer snow

do not be afraid of that doorstep and that street we used to go
it was only what it is
because the grammar of our bodies made it so

I could have broken the entire length of my life across your face
you were the language and the landscape and the place
if you had told me way back then
that after all that you'd be my friend
I would have laughed
held your heart in my fist
like light cut out of dark

and how your skin shone back then like Midas
touching rain that time you left me undone
your voice rang dissonant like a clashing sun
in the phosphorous frenzied blue
and this sky has not forgiven you
the streetlights remember too
the canopies of the trees on this street will not forget that place
and that absence you held up to my face
that took me instead of

you

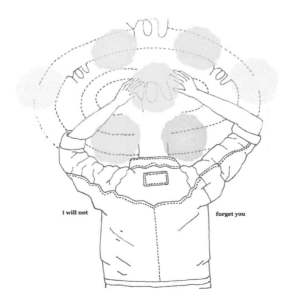

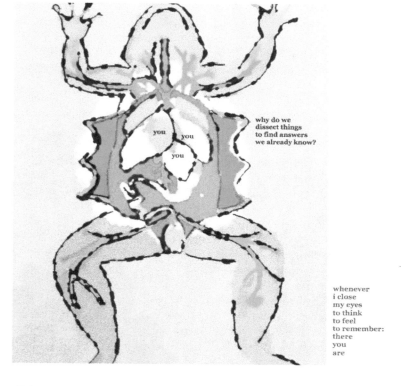

why do we
dissect things
to find answers
we already know?

whenever
i close
my eyes
to think
to feel
to remember:
there
you
are

CONCRETE: a surgery poem

I remember once getting an invite to
go on a tour of brutalist architecture
followed by light refreshments and a university lecture
on how the Soviets made any kind of softness obsolete
like it was a good thing that you could give them the sky
and they'd dip it in concrete

these are places where the damp scales the walls
like a memory you can't paint over
where the drains clog up and implode like confused supernovas
look
if you want a tour of brutalism
come and look around my body
I'll let you in for free

the segments of my spine like
breeze blocks burned from the inside out
graffiti and blue light and a broken-down lift and dirt in the
grout
all that limescale and yellow tape
stops the dreams from coming out
(that way, instead of blaming yourself
for the fact that your life is going nowhere
you can blame your upbringing for you never having got there)

sometimes the pain is so bad
I close my eyes and imagine taking an X-ray
my imagination has the power to turn my vertebrae opaque
and I can see my spine just sitting there
and I know it doesn't have eyes
but I feel it looking at me, berating me, saying
'please take better care of me
you're in charge of curating me and
you cannot build another me
I will not change or grow
you treat me like I'm disposable
you love me like I'm Lego
you're not young any more
let your baby gymnast dreams
go'

and I wonder,
was the surgeon witness to the sweetness
that my insides are missing?
so many holes for the filling
and not enough sugar to pour in
my skeleton bathes in sweetness
because that's the hue I choose to live in

I imagine watching him
the only man I've ever allowed in
preserving my old chest in glycerine
building me up different again
and I'm playing dead over my body

and he is hovering above me
time stretches the heart so thin
he can see where others have struck my skin
I don't need formaldehyde when I decide to die
it's in the fists of my bullies that I'll carry on living
and you're trying to pour all that sugar water in
but I'm telling you that regardless of you changing me
I'll be empty on the days I need to swim and
full on the days that I need the light to come in
so maybe if you cut my badness out
that'll be how the holiness gets in
and my skin is such a thin thing that's how the darkness gets in

surgery has made me feel the same way love does
somebody put their hands in me and gave me a good tidying up
I think there are two real ways of taking an internal photograph
fucking someone or opening them up
to be inside somebody is the worst and best kind of transgression
to break the boundary of the skin is
the ultimate act of possession

but at least for this kind I was unconscious
my pain emerged in subtitles
sometimes I think the only reason I know I'm alive
is because doctors are forced to check my vitals
my platelets dancing under the needle's wire
there's not much difference between love and fire but
at least you can control a
burn
when will people learn?

I am chaos on the inside
a blizzard in a swimming pool
an igloo filled with rain
on my worst days my
emptiness and heaviness taste exactly the same

I'm a playground where the astro
licks your knees with gravel glaze

I'm a closed-down pub with the sign still ablaze
a hollowed-out venue on a London estate

and when I was opened up all the past poured out
and now inside my chest there's a new house
in my heart's place and how beautiful it looks
how neat and tidy with its glossy paint
and detail and craftsmanship and care

but that's not safe to me
my memories don't live there

and I look around
I look around
I look around

there
you
aren't

BIG BANG: a painful poem

loving you filled my mouth with forest and alpine
you made me taste the same kind of magic that maybe
you only feel after watching Christmas films in July
or having birthday cake for breakfast hour
or eating oranges sat on the floor in the shower
juice pouring from your hands down your body like stars
sugared and sour
leaving you clean in the citrus landslide
blameless and whole and
crucified

from feeling

under the tight white cyanide
Rubik's brick ceramic slick

bathroom ceiling

once when I was young I was allowed wine at the table
and it made my little girl spine sit up straight
it felt like the dark grape was pulling my heart
right up through my mouth
the magic of altering how I felt just like that
that was what you did
like watching a compass in the Arctic suddenly fold south
loving you made me feel immense
it changed my tears from
pleas
to
evidence

you were the wish of a woman that the little girl in me needed

and when you left you burned every square inside me
right down to the ground
and the burning lit up my cells with a light so bright and so loud
that I still know there will never be a day

where the memory of you does not make
the very puzzle of me
feel set alight

you hurt me
but I apologised

destroying is not completion and
you can't make something right just by the act of abandonment
you can't separate atoms after quantum entanglement
and still after all these years I lie here
with the pieces missing and the control relinquished
and I am so very fucking lucky and yet

so utterly
unfinished

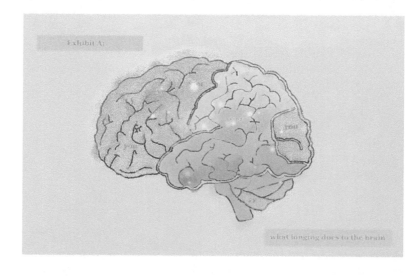

i cannot find find a filter that helps me forget you

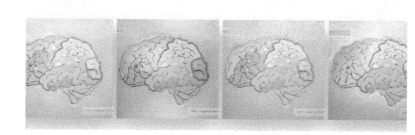

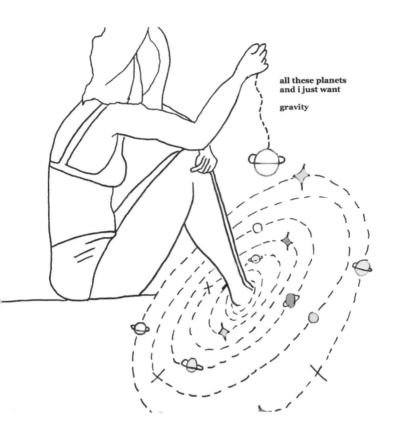

all these planets
and i just want

gravity

DAYDREAM: a wishing poem

I have daydreams that are my inner Narcissus
staring into the pool burning blue with my blisters
they are in love with their own bleach-bright reflections
their ghosts are perfect homes for my tidy projections
they are beautiful stones at the base of the lake
their trembling a controlled and tidy little earthquake

they're my weather, but they're worse because they last
and at least bad weather has a forecast
I can temper the rain because at least it comes with a warning

I stand, clinging on to them like a woman in mourning
a fragment of relief to stop me from feeling so low
no internal system gently reminding me to let them go

the brain has no pain receptors

there's a phrase that says
feed your dreams so that they can feed you
but my dreams
they leave me
starving
so what do I do when it's hunger they're carving?
and I wish just one time
my daydreams reminded me of the need to be alive
in the same way I need them to help me
forget it
it's like the magic keeps winning and I just sit there and let it

there's a fire between my legs like ember
I've got a daydream for that
reciprocity doesn't always last forever
I've got a daydream for that
you can't bring back the dead
I've got one for that too
but you can't change your lines without losing what's true
I'm addicted to their cosmic residue
I keep them archived away
I get them out on the blue days
but the problem is that every day is blue
and I'm starting to forget what is them and what's true
the addictive interplay of form
the metallic lustre of their power
the simple digraphic way that they fit inside an hour
and inside them I am paradise unfurling
but my pool is a frozen skin that's toxic and curdling
and only love pulls a plume into the glacier ice
it reminds me that outside them there still is life

but I have forgotten how to make authentic mistakes
these are my attempts to distance myself and to alienate

myself from what is true and difficult to integrate

the little girl in me is untucked at night
and my imagined realities hold her tight

in them I am a trapeze artist and a dragon slayer and I play rugby
I can break into pirouettes or punches
depending on which way the circus and the world needs
I'm a pianist with the keys
scattering under my scrutiny like confetti
I have straight A's and am shy about my accolades
and size eight and captain of the hockey team
I have eyes greener than mine now that dance darkly
ivy caught in a rainstorm
a mysterious genius since the day I was born

I have no dreams where I help young people
or where I am kind or where I'm a writer
it's like I've disowned myself
all petrol, no lighter
I'm constantly waiting to ignite
waiting to tear open the night
my daydreams are distractions holding me tight
my kisses no substance and all magic and all gloss

the brightest waxed apple in the basket
is always the most bitter because
it's the one that shines not for its taste but because of its finish
see
my dreams are the polish on the ordinary shoe of me
it doesn't matter how many things I think or try to be
I could be a famous academic or a model or an athlete
I could be a mother or a painter or a queen
lose four stone, get my jaw filed down
rearrange my organs and turn my heart the wrong way round

I still
would not
want
me

THERAPIST: a calling poem

before we start speaking about things
let me at first state the obvious point
that I have mental health problems and I see the dark
and so me being somebody to help you fix yours
makes you laugh
and that having mental health issues and becoming a therapist
is somewhat ironic
but you don't tell a mechanic who keeps fixing her own car
that her doing so is 'iconic'
so why do they say it to me?

I don't know much, but I know minds
I know them
I walk around in them and I sit in their spare rooms
and I watch how they burn down the windows
of the towns they reside in
I know how to help people learn how to fix them
but appreciate them even more for what's broken inside them
for the cracks where they fortify the doors
just make more layers for their inhabitants to explore

I know how one tiny little thing
can shut off the electricity for days
and you're stumbling around in the dark but people are shouting
'turn the light on'
and you shout
'there's no electricity'
and so they
shout
'TRY
HARDER'

but if they're clueless
then they make the mistake of blaming your walls
as though you were the one who built them
and they're not a sum of the hands of your makers
why do they blame you for your bricks instead of your creators?

maybe people weren't meant to be houses
maybe we were meant to be
gardens
where it is acceptable for small deaths to happen every day
in order to make things grow
why don't people understand
you cannot separate the bud from the root
or the rot from the fruit?
they come together
but I can't find a metaphor for that happening
inside a home

maybe it just takes someone to say
that whoever laid your pipes and wires was tired that day
and don't you know
houses can't fix themselves on their own?
they need electricians to make the house
back into a home

I am in love with my electrician
every night my partner lights a lantern in me
even though most days the wick is worn to ash, and
every time it's dark I shout at her
'NO HOPE' and she never shouts at me to try
but still she ignites the trip switch
and even if not all the lights work
at least some work well enough
for her to navigate me to the stairs

sometimes I can't find the lights for you either
but I promise to
hold your hands and help you get
to a place where sleep comes softly

because I know how to hold a hand
that's covered in cuts and bruises
and not be scared of the cosmos that leaks out of the skin
I am not scared of your pain
I am not scared of thirty-five missed calls again and again

at the bridge
and chunks of hair in hands and a neck wrapped in cords
fingernails being pulled off
and phone calls with police officers and doctors and landlords
I know that sometimes dancing with death
is the only way to make the noise seem quieter, and you
are a beautiful dancer
and even though I know what it is like
to inhabit the hell of your skin
I won't ever tell you that death is the answer

I just want you to remember that it won't be dark in your home
not if I'm
there with you
let's build a street where the walls are doors
and the sky is orange and the ground is blue
where we all learn how to be electricians for ourselves
and, even better, where we learn
how to build walls that can hold us
we can use the dark to guide us
and light the lamps that blaze inside us
then we won't need our houses any more

we will make houses out of our bones and skin
we will have our home within

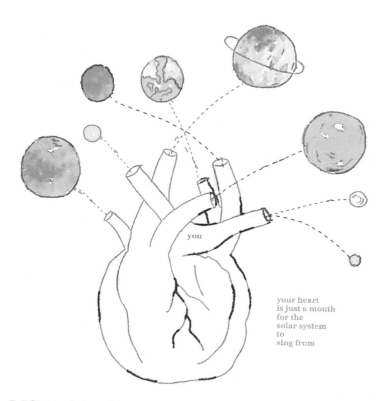

you

your heart
is just a mouth
for the
solar system
to
sing from

LIST: a bipolar poem

lately life feels less like a prize
more like an endurance exercise
with a pain that won't go
a pain I cannot euthanise
and my feelings flux and change
so much throughout a single day
that sometimes I am amazed
that none of my friends hear my sadness vibrate
we are getting to the point where
the branches of our trees are growing apart
and I know that I share roots with most of them
but they weigh heavy on my heart
and we are all busy trudging towards
our own private horizon in our own private walls

and these days I am struggling to see
the good in them all

I have become the mirror held up to their inner Narcissus
hear them say to me
'Beth, we are soul sisters
so sit and listen to my stories of how life has left me with blisters'
and I just want to say
let's talk about how the good life missed us
(there is something about sisters that seems so vicious)

talk about why people deliver their work in a spoken-word
voice
it's like they have to deliver their work in the way
that alienates people without giving them a choice
I'm not going to spit from the origins of my umbilical
waxing lyrical about what I think is a miracle
coming from my mouth
because the real shit that I feel goes on down south
and my life is ordinary, and beautiful, and awkward
and stunning, and often so very boring
some days it is like the mouth of hell is yawning open
and night is drawing to a close and I suppose
I want to perform tonight, but for what?
for my ego?
so I can say to my mama
'I performed in another venue you know'?
and I've lost it
my grace
the thing that made me feel good about writing in the first place
I don't enjoy a single thing any more

not even this
so the doctor gave me a list

he looked up a list of six things
you're supposed to do when you're depressed
he tells me he knows that this list must be 'true'
because he found it on the internet

here it is
the thing that is supposed to cure me is this

*Number one: Accompany someone to the movies, a concert or a small
get-together*

I can't watch movies without feeling like someone
has turned me inside-out and distorted me like a rumour
and my heart is stapled to my skin like a TGI Friday's badge
a cheap blazing neon tumour
my heart is killing me
how can I feed it with more dark?
so don't give me art
because I don't need anything else to make me feel, please
a concert?
you think I have the strength to stand?
darling, I am on my knees
every day I am on my knees
so how can I go to parties?
they crush me
I can't even find the strength to sit
in the toilet upstairs with the door locked behind me
and when you talk to me I see your lips moving
but you have become an alien to me
all I do is think about how I can leave out the back door
without someone noticing me
the space I leave behind me is smaller
than the void that I exacerbate
take my absence any day over the goodness my body annihilates
take me as negative space as I try to recover from the hurt I
create
that apparently is purely of my own doing

Number two: Have a coffee and talk to someone about your feelings

thank you for suggesting that I talk to a friend
believe it or not I had thought of it before
but talking to most of my friends is like banging on a locked
door

at the gates of hell
like looking into dead eyes and finding
no life inside there any more
because I need them to be my strength
because I can't do it on my own
and most of my twenties have been spent blind
to the fact that I am the only person I can call home
that even when I am comfortable I'm really just
sleeping on a sinkhole
how can I tell you that coffee makes me feel manic?
I feel all my synapses snapping and crackling
like candy millions in my blood, like panic
how can I tell you that seeing that you have rung
fills me with dread because it means that I have to call you back
and I cannot handle the pressure of that?

Number three: Read a book

read a book? look
I think that it is books that got me into trouble in the first place
reading about how maybe we are all in a dream
and we are just insignificant in outer space
if you want a recipe for depression
mix in existentialism with fiction and then
tell me that your brain doesn't get weighed down in friction
this is an affliction of ideals
that we are nothing and made of atoms and stardust
governed by lust and love and all in between
yet we are encouraged to pay our bills and make our beds
and keep our homes well painted and clean
how do any of you deal with the dissonance of that?
how can I read about a thousand different lives and truth
when I cannot even stare at myself in the mirror
and separate my own pain from all of you?
I don't need another story
I need to learn how to run a bath
and wash up without my hands shaking
I need to learn the art of forgiving
as all the while my bones break inside my skin

with the sadness and the weight of all the lives I am not living

Number four: Call or email an old friend

they're old friends for a reason

Number five: Go for a walk with a workout buddy

I told you I am on my knees
and you expect me to take my body through its physical peak?
I love to swim and to be in the water
but I do not have the energy to lift my hands to my head, you see
to tuck my hair into a swimming hat
and to pull the Lycra over my form
and then go up and down day after wretched day
and then get out of the mint-blue warm
and take my costume off
and then wash my hair and then condition it
and then put moisturiser on and deodorant
and then dry my body
the shattering tediousness of it
and put on my underwear and dry my hair and get dressed
I have fucked up self-motivation with all the rest
I cannot put on my shoes and then my makeup
and then walk home and try hard not to think
how can I do that when I do not even know
how I am going to get through the next blink?

Number six: Confide in a clergy member, therapist or teacher

I used to teach at a Catholic school
and they were obsessed with converting me
how many times can you say 'get your rosaries off my ovaries'?
I don't need confession for punishment
being in my body is punishment enough
and I don't need the threat of hell because I'm in it now
nothing could be worse than this
I've pulled out my eyelashes so there's no more chances to wish

and I don't need a Bible to make me feel ashamed
of what I have become
how many times can I tell you the last time I spoke to a teacher
she had sex with me and pinned down my arms
like she was a hurricane and I was the sea
and now my body is covered in waves
from where she used her lightning hands to touch me?
I do not trust a single figure in authority
five therapists in a row
have told me that I am too ill for them to help me

there are two things that rhyme with the name Beth
and those words are breath and death
typical that my name only works in a poem with
what life begins with and how it ends

so I take your six things on this fucking list and I raise you a life
I am only still here because of medication
and the way my girlfriend folds me away every night
like I am a letter and she is an envelope
and I am safe even though
I do not know where I am going
where I am being sent

if I will ever get there, in the end

sometimes I wish I had never met her
because I know at some point one of us
will be without the other in body
and I don't want to be dead without her
she promised if she goes first she will get heaven ready for me
she promised me that she would keep my cloud warm for me
she holds me so tight that she makes the sideways come out of
me
I never knew love had the power to italicise me

sometimes I love her so much I can't stand it
and I have to go outside
and scream at the sky in the middle of the day

and I go all fifty shades of cray
because I want to take a mould to her head
and cast her skull out of plaster of Paris and clay
in case she dies
so there is never a time in this universe
when I will be without the shape of her head in my hands

can you try to understand?
your list makes me feel tiny
your list makes me feel like I am a book with no structure
just words spat on a page
that don't make sense
and the comma is just a break in the life sentence
and it's the wrong story for the wrong age
I just want to find a way to get through the days
without feeling like my insides are dissolving
under depression's gaze
I don't want to feel tired any more
I just want to feel okay

VAN GOGH: a painting poem

when I was five I ran myself a bath up to half
and filled the rest with ice
I wanted to make my outsides feel colder
than the winter that I felt sparkling dark inside

there was a painting by Van Gogh hanging above the hallway
and it glowed at night
I looked up in my encyclopaedia that sunflowers love the light
and I pressed the painting under my fingers
and made a wish with all my might
and when it didn't come true
I cried
I didn't know how to crack through the sky
I didn't know that it was a print on the wall
to me it was the real thing
and it made me feel brave and it made me feel small
and I always wished for the same thing in my head
I wished to bring people back from the dead

but meanwhile there was normal life to be getting on with
after it happened Mum still took me to WH Smith
in the stationery aisle
for things to be proud about when we went back to school
I always begged for the special pens
that smelled like lemons and grapes
bruised peaches and neon swimming pools
but I would sob in the aisles because I was never allowed
the pencils that smelled of these countries far away
(so I rubbed sugar with spit on my pens
and dreamed them to be sweet like fruit
in my own special way)
the grape pencils smelled the way I imagined
summer camp in the movies would smell
like lip balm and lake water
and the acid tang of lips tasting sun cream
but my summers weren't like that
and I hated the pictures my pens made
because they never quite measured up to my dreams

there's a difference between being pushed away and being set free

everybody went away to tropical faraway places
that smelled like the pencils
in Cuban lime and Persian pink
but my heart was stuck inside the sunflower house
and my room got so hot in the summer
and there was nowhere to go or to escape or to think
so I felt trapped and it made my chest hurt
and everything felt black that I touched
and there was no black pencil in the set I wanted
only sweet cola brown
(and not even that
because Mum said the set cost too much)

I used to hope the painting could talk to me
say, 'I'm sorry
I too was painted by someone in the wrong body
It wasn't supposed to be this way
we both aren't well because someone accidentally put you
in the wrong day in the wrong decade'
I don't know what it is like to be a different person
or to have a different life
but even when we flew on an aeroplane
to somewhere really far away to explore
I would feel so sad that even though it was hot
I was still the same person I was before
there aren't enough flowers to make up for that
not enough sunflowers to make you a thing to be forgot
not enough paintings in the world to hide
the dark of the walls and the damp and the rot

everybody in the neighbourhood would stare at my legs
when the weather was nice
because they were so pale that they were a bluish white
you can see a vein in them
and when I am hot or self-conscious
it throbs left and right like ink under light

and I can see my skin move around it
like Vincent's stems and leaves keeping me surrounded
the vein leaves me dumbfounded because it reminds me

I am here

seeing the insides of my body move like that
seeing my blood blaze blue under my skin so clear
I don't know if I could ever be brave enough
to cut off my entire ear
but I do know this much
is true
I would lay down the light
for you

there is a space at the end of the solar system called the
heliosphere
and scientists say that if you took one breath there
your lungs would turn to dust
and when I was little on Sundays
there was a space between suppertime and bedtime
where my insides ached like the edge of the world
like heat and light in internal combust

I used to spend hours up in the trees as a kid and I was so bored
so bored so bored so bored
that I would bite my tongue until I could taste
iron coins in my mouth and blood in my throat
I used to curl up in bed with a massive pile of cushions
wrapped tightly up in a great big coat
and pretend and pretend that there were real hands
holding me like it was the end
with my sugared pencils and leftover roast dinners
and veins in my legs that would throb and bend
and I would dream of a woman to take me away from all of this
a lover to take me away from all this with a kiss
and in my mind when she held me I could taste sunflowers
for the first time since it all
I would know what tasting a colour would feel like

and in the dictionary it says
heliotropism is the term that describes how sunflowers' faces
always follow the light as it journeys across the sky
extracts from the flower are used to remove
contamination from nuclear disasters
it can neutralise uranium and lead
it removes toxicity from water and earth
and removes the matter that is dead

I think the painting was a metaphor for you
the sunflower
that lives
inside
my
head

it's not as simple as dividing us up into
who was wrong and who was right
it was more a matter of who could fight
their dark with light better
and I followed the formula right down to the very letter
I would run baths made of ice
to make my outsides as cold as I felt inside
I wasn't allowed gum
so I chewed Blu Tack and when I was caught I lied
I wasn't allowed a bikini
so I chopped my swimming costume in half
I wasn't allowed to smile
so I laughed

adding sugar and spit to the tip of my tongue

dreaming of you coming in
to bend
my dimension

longing for you
in the quiet dark

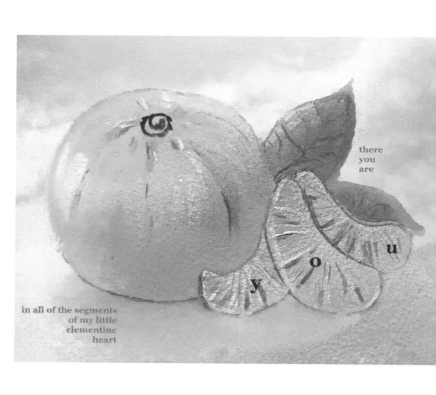

there
you
are

y o u

in all of the segments
of my little
clementine
heart

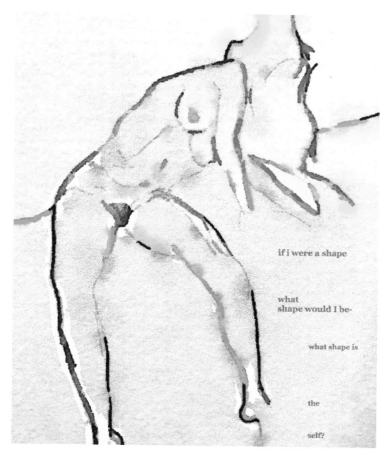

if i were a shape

what
shape would I be-

what shape is

the

self?

I
am
so
sick
of
being
defined
by
my
body

WINDOWSILL: a plant poem

even plants have muscle memory
they know their limits
they know how high they can grow before they need to stop
and I don't like remembrance days because
they excuse all the days where we forgot
I don't like that the dead receive more flowers
than they ever did when they were alive
I don't like that we buy flowers
to hide the shame of the fact that we
never met our friends at their doorway
to stand with them by their windows
underneath the sill of what is forgotten
with handfuls of eucalyptus
and dandelions with seeds soft as cotton
we never said
'these are for you
and they are for no other reason
than the fact that you are alive in this world
at exactly the same time I am, and that
that feels like a privilege
you look just like love
what a time, darling
what a time to be
alive'

THIRTEEN:
the things depression has taught me

1) Maybe your illness is a normal response to a society that is broken. Maybe it is actually the world that is sick, not you. It is okay to have needs. If you do not know how to meet your own needs yet, that is also okay. If you created maladaptive coping mechanisms to help you survive when you were little, then that's not something to be ashamed of. That is something to be proud of. In spite of it all, you kept going. You could not possibly have met your own needs when you were a child. If there were such a thing as a child that could meet their own needs, then the world wouldn't need teachers and therapists. If you disappear inside your daydreams or if your fingernails leave pink crescent moons on your skin, if you don't eat for the day just to feel silence on your insides, if you open up your skin to try to let the dark out and the light in, then you are brave. At the bottom of every drink and the tip of every syringe is just a desperate plea to find out how to live with less pain. There are other ways to do this, I promise. You only seek to quieten the hurt because you refuse to harden your heart. This does not make you weak; it makes you extraordinary.

2) Do not measure your trauma against the trauma of another. Trauma is not only an occurrence but an absence too. Sometimes the things that are missing hurt more than what is seen. When somebody calls you with happy news, you do not say, 'Don't be too happy, as someone somewhere is happier,' so do not do the same with sadness. Every time you diminish your experience, you hinder your growth. If you try to be selfless, it will not work. Selflessness will make you selfish because it means that you will have to rely on others to pick up your broken bits when they come tumbling out of you. Your trauma does not need witnesses to be validated when the only person who can really see it for how badly it hurt you is you. Learn to let your eyes be enough. Love yourself enough to feel comfortable to be misunderstood.

3) Psychiatric wards are not like holidays. The bedding is not soft; there are no rain showers or views of wild forests. You are not cradled by a nurse who could be a mother figure, nobody rubs the hurt bruise of your back in parental circular motions, you are not treasured like a baby, you are not unusual. They are not the answer – merely a holding pen to get you chemically stable. Chemical stability and inner peace are not always the same. Do not go looking for nirvana inside a hospital ward, and do not make friends with your demons. I know these demons have held you with so much tenderness for nearly all of your life, but they do not love you. They are strange ghosts inside familiar clothes. Do not keep running back to them just because they are the only safe place that you know.

4) I often tell my psychiatrist that I wish that I went purple. That way people could see and they would say, 'Oh my goodness – why are you in work? You are so purple,' or even 'Time to rest today, angel, you are purple,' or maybe 'You did all this whilst you were purple? You are incredible.' And nobody would imply that you could undo the purple with positive thinking, or yoga, or supplements. Nobody would try to wash the purple from your body, because they would know that nothing that exists could remove it apart from time. This won't ever happen in our lifetime, nor will there be a blood test that shows our tears so we can wave it in the faces of the sceptics. That is okay. There is no blood test that shows the colour of compassion either, but I know that it goes hand in hand with the ability to feel pain. I don't believe in heaven, but I believe in kindness, and sometimes I think those two things are the same. You cannot prove those things either, and yet they are the reason most of us get out of bed.

5) This illness is your context, but it is not your fault. Everybody loves the quote that says 'broken crayons still colour the same' but forgets the fact that in order to do this they need to be held differently. The only person who can hold you with the amount of concentration and empathy and tenderness that you need is you. But be patient and don't be too hard on yourself. Carrying a burden does not make you one. We all have times when we feel we are trapped on the wrong side of the mirror. The only difference is that you have the bravery to both experience and express it. Emotions can't hurt you, but the things you do to avoid them can. Please remember this.

6) There is a whale called Whale 52, and he is described as the loneliest whale in the world because he calls out to the sea in a different frequency from the others. This means that his kind cannot hear or understand him. Remember that even though the whales cannot hear him, other creatures can. There is no such thing as a being who has a cry that is unrecognisable across all species. You are not the exception. You will find your people.

7) The same tree that you read underneath, making bracelets from its blossoms, may be the tree that one day is your casket, and neither of you knows it yet. One cannot exist without the other. Do not be afraid of what is coming. Don't close your eyes to death. It is here and it happens and it is part of it all. Do not be afraid of dying, only of not living. They are not the same thing.

8) Do not rely on deep connections with people just because they are able to help you regulate your emotions. You need to learn the art of self-regulation. They won't teach you this in school because they want you to believe that if you are obedient and you buy nice things and work your whole life for a big house then you will be okay. These things will not make you okay. We are taught that we are only worthwhile if we are productive. Empathy isn't good for the economy, but don't let that stop you from loving the very ground that holds you up each day. Keep learning. If you have to learn about something terrible because you have never experienced it yourself, please consider that not a chore but a privilege. Awareness without motion is just a pseudonym for pain. Action what you learn, even if the action you choose is not to act. Make your happiness deliberate if you can.

9) A good therapist will save your life. A brilliant therapist will teach you how to save your own. Do not rely on a professional to fix you. Seeking external tenderness to counteract internal brutality is a recipe for disaster. However, if you find the right people, they can model for you what it is to be both soft and strong. My psychiatrist has a gentle voice and wears tropical-coloured socks and has a hammock in his garden. He makes me feel safe. My therapist has impossible blue eyes and wears beautiful dresses and lives in a giant dolls' house surrounded by trees. She is nurturing and ferocious and she makes me feel brave. She told me that she cannot lead me out of the woods but that she can walk alongside me when I am lost amongst it all. She is teaching me to be curious about my emotions instead of afraid. Every time I see them both I feel like I'm being given the gift of seeing myself properly for the first time. Try to find the people who can help you to angle your mirror so that it leans back towards you with something less like judgement and more like forgiveness.

10) Caterpillars are warm and safe inside their cocoons for weeks and weeks. Butterflies live for only a few days, but they get to fly. If you don't know which one to choose, choose flying. When you walk past a pigeon, remember that even the things you think are ordinary have remarkable stories. Pigeons can see ultraviolet light, which means they can see colours that we as humans don't even know exist. There is no such thing as a living thing that is not remarkable. This applies to you too.

11) Your imagination can make the celestial out of a cul-de-sac. Every kiss translated into a tight little sunrise. Your daydreams are beautiful, but be careful not to stay inside them. Notice instead how the bubbles in the washing-up look like stars, how the laundry holds hands in the tumble dryer, how a leaf curls shyly when it is thirsty. This, right now in front of us, is all that we have. Pay attention. Sometimes people will not have been what you needed. Do not invent an alternative narrative. What happened has happened. It has made you you.

12) Do not create a love story and stamp it on the heart of another and allow them to do the same to you. Mutual projection is not love. Sitting quietly and allowing somebody their space is. There is no such thing as a happily-ever-after. Never put your tools and paintbrushes away; there is always work to do. This is what makes life beautiful.

13) Nobody can be in your skin or live for you. The magic you are looking for is in the work that you are avoiding. Make your bed and shower every day, even if it is like lugging your bones through a nightmare. This may be all you can do. Sit under the shower and try to imagine it washing away all of the broken in you. Turn the lights out and have some Lucozade under the faucet and imagine you're in a spa and a mama has given you stars to drink. Remember that somewhere a flower is actually breaking out of concrete.

You will too.

This book is for my army:

For all the teenagers and children I have ever taught, looked after, cared for and learned from. You have all taught me about kindness, laughter and forgiveness. It has been my privilege and honour to work with you.

For my writer friends who believed in me when my poems were scribbles done in eye liner on receipts: Andrea Spisto, Antony Owen, Carrie J Lyell, Caroline Teague, David Lee Morgan, David Morley, Dion Power, Ernesto Sarezale, Hannah Gordon, the powerhouse that is Lisa Luxx, Matthew Jockel, Maureen Freely, Megan Chapman, Michael Hulse, Pat Cash and Trudy Howson. Thank you also to Bridget Hart and Clive Birnie at Burning Eye for making this possible for me.

For the incredible men in my life (you show me how to be safe): Adam Russell, Arun Teji, Cherinor Deen Jalloh, Christopher Beggs, Chris D'Souza, Dean Goldfarb, my hubby Gregory Williams, my adopted son Nate Jittu, Nick Tipple, Simon Cox, Tim Renouf and Tindy Adegaba.

For the incredible women in my life (you show me how to be brave): Alarissa Nicholas, Alicia Fletcher, Amy Deane, Bernadette Kavanagh, Bex Reid, Carolyn Goodfellow, Carrie Biddulph, Charlotte Hickmore, Charlotte Levy, Cherry Cant, Dale Tyus, Dolly Alderton, Emma Thompson, Eve Burton, Gen Bissett, Hannah Evans, Holly Bidgood, Jen Dennis, Jessica Hinds, Judy Bidgood, Jules Carey, Kat Mann, Kelly Tuite, Kerry Sindewald, Laura Boyd, Leela Trikamji, Lily Robert, Lisa Bennett, Lisa Cowell, Luce Bidwell, Lucy Hall, Lucy Hayton, Peta Kilian, Philippa Kavanagh, Rose Cant, Ruby Hall, Samantha Howlett, Sarah Saleh, Terri Power, Tish Faust and Yasmin McManus.

For my warriors (you show me how to be strong): Alison Dace, Annabelle Crick, Becky Crossweller, Becky French, Becky Roche, Clae Eastgate, Elaine Mitchell, Jo Croucher, Josephine Exley, Katy Ashworth, Lizzie Eyre, Nicola Butler, Nina Haefele, Polly Bennett, Rocky Clarke, Rosie Hawkins and Zoe Chiswick.

For my mamas (you show me how to be treasured- you helped me keep going): Clare Wise, Emma Kennedy, Jessica Berson, Julie Rogers, Laura Osman, Lesley Morris, Philippa Madams, Rachel Kingdon-Saxby and Saskia Russell.

For my soul food (you show me how to be loving- you helped my heart stay open): Abbey Smithcliffe, Alexandra Green, Alex Jones, Charlie Gavshon-Kirkbride, Charlotte Dubery, Jessica Murrain, Lucy Drewett, Nicola Valvis, Rachel Nwkoro and Rosi Croom.

For my sisters (you show me how to be soft- you helped me fall in love with living): Annabel Norbury, Christabel Cant, my platonic wife Gemma Penford, Kyla MacDonald, Sarah Worboys and Victoria Fischer.

For my guardians (you show me the light and the way- you helped guide me): Andrew Margo, Rachel Dickinson, Sandra Tapie for showing me so much love and compassion over the years, Suzy Byrne, and my nurturing, clever and kind therapist Caroline Midgley. Caroline, you saved my life and taught me how to save my own in the process. Working with you has profoundly altered me and you are extraordinary.

For my pets and those of my friends and family (you show me joy and love- my love for you is unconditional): My guinea pigs, my darling Bug and best boy Smudge, and our babies; Reuben and Coconut; my world.

For my family far and wide (you show me how to be true) Anna Abdulai, Paul and Lesley Thomson, Caroline Thomson, Uncle Kevin, Auntie Lyn. Auntie Cheryl, Uncle Kevin, Freddie and Grace; Auntie Anna, Uncle Greg, Lucia, Jordan, Marnia and Rob. Grandma, Grandad, Uncle Ray and Auntie Val. My magical Grandpa and my dearest friend and inspiration; my Nanny Nora.

For my family close and near (you show me home): My witty and powerful twin Joshua, my warm and kind sister in law Jilly, my fabulous and funny Madres, and my treasured perfect baby Sammy- my little brother and my bestest boy, my sweet angel.

For the future (you show me hope): My little sister Ella 'Panda' Iredale, Elodie Crossweller Martin, baby starfish Mimi Rose Joan D'Souza, Monty Cox, Poppy Neelands, Raphael Jeary, Merlin and Wilder Dann, Sienna Smithcliffe, my godson Roderick Broderick, and my niece Baby Isla Aspen Rose, our beautiful Lala: you babies will always be surrounded by a perfect sunbeam of love straight from my heart that will always keep you all warm- this is my promise to you. You can come to me for anything and for as long as I am here I will love and nurture you.

For my hero (you show me magic): my Papa, my Daddio, my protector- you light up a room: you hold me and you keep me safe. All that I am, you taught me.

For my great, truest love (you show me my heart- it is in awe of yours- you are the pink peonies and the turquoise swimming pools and the solar storms and the glitter in the anthracite and the curve of the moon and all of the golden great good things): Cc.

Cc- I love you. You're the neon x

Lightning Source UK Ltd.
Milton Keynes UK
UKHW021018181120
373616UK00004B/10